# Modern Methodism in England
## 1932–1998

Exploring Methodism

# Modern Methodism in England
# 1932–1998

John Munsey Turner

EPWORTH PRESS

0 7162 0512 2

First published 1998
by Epworth Press
20 Ivatt Way, Peterborough PE3 7PG

Typeset at The Spartan Press,
Lymington, Hants
and printed in Great Britain by
Redwood Books, Trowbridge, Wilts

# Contents

## System of references

A book like this draws upon a wide range of source material, and this brief note explains how, it is hoped, interested readers will be helped to go behind the text to the evidence.

1. Direct quotations are handled in two ways: sometimes by being placed in a numbered box, where full bibliographical information is supplied, and sometimes by being footnoted in the usual way. In both cases, the details provided should lead straightforwardly to the original source.

2. The many *Reports* to the Methodist Conference and *Statements* by the Methodist Conference which are cited can all be found in the *Agenda* of the Conference in the year specified, and the most important have been collected and published separately: for details, see Suggestions for Further Reading.

3. The many books which are mentioned but not quoted are listed alphabetically, with full details, in the Bibliography.

4. The list of books suggested for Further Reading concentrates on pointing readers to necessary background information.

# Preface to the Series

What is Methodism and how did it begin? What did John Wesley teach? We sing Charles Wesley's hymns but what can we discover about his life? What is the character and work of the Methodist Church today? What have Methodists had to say about social issues? What place have women had in Methodism? These are the kind of questions which *Exploring Methodism* is aiming to answer.

All the contributors are experts in their field, and all write in an attractive way that will appeal to both church members and everyone interested in the life and history of the churches. The format of the books enables each writer to introduce extracts from the writings of the main characters and official church documents, and in this way to bring the reader close to what was actually said and written by the leaders of the church and church members. It is hoped that the books will be studied in house groups and other discussion groups as well as read by individuals, and questions for discussion, directly related to the present day, are included at the end of each chapter. Each volume contains an annotated list of books for further reading.

Barrie Tabraham opened the series with a general overview of Methodist history, concentrating on the origins and early development. In the present volume John Munsey Turner traces the life and thinking of the Methodist Church and its leaders and members since Methodist Union in 1932 up to the present day, and takes a look into the future. Forthcoming volumes will cover the life and work of Charles Wesley, Methodist theology, Methodist devotion, music in Methodism, official statements by the Church on social and political issues, the activity of women in early Methodism, Methodist preachers and preaching, and other topics.

C. S. Rodd

# Foreword

John Turner is a brave man! Methodist historians tend to concentrate on well-documented periods before 1900 which can more easily be interpreted in time's perspective. To discern patterns in the confusing twentieth century is much more difficult. John has already given us thoroughly documented and perceptive studies of Methodism and ecumenism up to 1982 and of English Methodism from 1900 to 1932. Now he completes the story up to the present. At the risk of embarrassing him, I would suggest that John himself represents much of what has been best in modern Methodism. On the one hand a scholarly and liberal (yet properly chastened and biblical) evangelicalism, sensitive to the modern world. On the other hand a deep affection and commitment to the local church and its people – who often figure in this book. Few are better qualified to give a well-informed and balanced picture of Methodism's variety, achievements, shortcomings and future prospects. The story is told in a lively style and deftly set in its wider social context and in relation to other churches. I warmly commend the book to Methodists who wish to know what their church has achieved and where it is going. It will, perhaps, be even more informative to non-Methodists puzzled by this strange blend of rule-book and spontaneity, personal religion and social concern which was inherited from John Wesley and still has something to offer to church and society today.

Henry D. Rack

# Preface

Dr E. J. Hobsbawm in his recent survey of what he calls the Short Twentieth Century 1914–1991 says: 'The destruction of the past or rather of the social mechanisms that link one's contemporary experience to that of earlier generations, is one of the most characteristic and eerie phenomena of the late twentieth century. Most young men and women at the century's end grow up in a sort of permanent present lacking any organic relation to the public past of the times they live in. This makes historians, whose business it is to remember what others forget, more essential at the end of the second millennium than ever before.'[1] Hobsbawm also admits that his history writing is always influenced by the sight, as a teenager in Berlin, of Adolf Hitler becoming Chancellor of the Third Reich in 1933. Any consideration of the life of the church would be irrelevant, if we forget that our age is the 'era of violence' of Hitler and Stalin, of Apartheid and the IRA, and of the rise and decline of Marxism as a world faith as well as of the ecumenical and liturgical movements. Any history of Methodism in this period must take account of the world in which we have lived.

I was baptized in 1930, became a Sunday school member in 1935 and, I suppose, have been 'in connexion' with Methodism ever since, a product of the Methodist Association of Youth Clubs and Cambridge University Methodist Society. Being a circuit minister from 1956 onwards has taken me to Colchester, Burton upon Trent, Sheffield, a university chaplaincy in Leeds, a tutorship at the Queen's College Birmingham from 1970 to 1981 and then circuit superintendency in Halifax and Bolton from 1981 to 1994. So I write from practical experience of the life of the church in the turmoil of a rapidly changing and sometimes very bewildering world. I try to be accurate and fair to those with whom I sometimes have profoundly disagreed. Contemporary history is an enormously risky business. I can only tell it as I see it and as I have lived it. The late Rupert Davies was a constant encourager and honest critic of my earlier historical enterprises. Our generation owe more than we can say to scholars like him and Gordon Rupp. We do well not to forget their vision both of what Methodism could be and of a wider church to which we belong. So I offer this in their memory, and to the ordinary people of 'grassroots' Methodism who get a mention here.

John Munsey Turner

# I
# Introduction

## Methodism then and now

A good way of 'doing' history is to begin where you are and ask 'How did we become what we are?' Go into the nearest town or city centre. You will find the parish church or cathedral, often going back to the Middle Ages before the Reformation. In my home town a statue of a Saxon princess marks the land she gave for the church. You will probably find a Roman Catholic church established during the renewal of that church in the last century. There may also be a Friends' Meeting House where Quakers have met for their largely silent, prayerful worship for two or three centuries. In a big town there could be a Methodist Central Hall, dating from the turn of the century when there was a 'Forward Movement' in Methodism expressing a great concern for the poor of the large cities. The 'Hall' will probably be used for all sorts of civic and educational events – the United Nations, for example, had its first Assembly in Westminster Central Hall. Look at any Methodist church built before Methodist Union in 1932: it may well be inscribed 'Wesleyan Methodist' or 'Primitive Methodist' or if you live in the South West or the Isle of Wight, 'Bible Christian'. Who on earth were they? What *were* our grandparents up to? Go into a Methodist church. Why is the pulpit central? Look at the hymn books. Why are so many hymns by Charles Wesley? However contemporary or 'state of the art' we think we are, we are the product of history, and it can be fascinating to explore it. But we begin *now*.

Methodism is one of the largest Protestant communions making a notable contribution to the world church at all levels. It is very strong in the United States. If there is a 'special relationship' between Britain and the USA, Methodism is a significant part of it, and, indeed, one cause of it. Methodism is small but vigorous in South America; strong in parts of West, South and East Africa; strong in the Pacific Islands like Tonga; small but not entirely overshadowed by Lutherans and the Reformed traditions in Europe, including the former Soviet Union; and united, though not in its American forms, with other communions in North and South India, Pakistan, Canada, Australia and France.

This is all the result of two prongs of mission from Great Britain and the USA. In Great Britain there are almost 400,000 members – more than those who belong to the Labour Party or watch football league matches, though not much more than half the number when Methodist Union took place in 1932. In England Methodism has prepared twice for unity and ultimate union with other churches with the goal of 'one church renewed for mission'. Now Methodism is still on its own, though it has a place in many Local Ecumenical Partnerships in which there is a sharing of buildings and ministry. It seeks a renewed confidence in evangelism, a mission alongside the poor as well as the lower and middle class which it had some part in fostering.

So let's look at the past through the eyes of the present. Who are we? Where did we come from?

## 1. Who were the Methodists?

What jobs have been held by the last three generations of your family? My father was a local government officer, my grandfathers a harness maker and an engineer, and my great-grandfathers a shoe maker, an ostler, a worker in an iron works and a shopkeeper. They were very typical of the people Methodism has attracted.

In an analysis of Methodism in his *England in the Eighteenth Century*, Sir John Plumb stated: 'By 1760 Methodism was easily the most co-ordinated body of opinion in the country, the most fervent, the most dynamic. Had it been bent on revolution in Church or State nothing could have stopped it. But then Methodism was not a religion *of* the poor but *for* the poor'.[1] There is both truth and exaggeration here. John Wesley (1703–1791) was able in a remarkable way to bridge the gulf between the Age of Reason and the 'folk religion' of the poor. He certainly felt more at home with the poor than with the rich, and left the offer of the gospel to the aristocracy to Lady Huntingdon and her largely Anglican allies. But though Wesley had great sympathy with those at the bottom of the heap, his helpers never recruited large numbers of what Karl Marx was to call the 'lumpen proletariat'. Wesley's message, in fact, fuelled the aspirations of the artisan class, the skilled workers who were later to be called the 'labour aristocracy' and formed the bureaucracies which followed in the wake of urbanization. Methodism had a majority of its members in this group – and indeed still has, with its army of clerks, nurses, teachers, and engineers, and its sprinkling of accountants and other representatives of a somewhat more affluent middle class.

Wesley's Methodism – whatever he may have said about the dangers of affluence and wealth – had a discipline which appeals to the aspiring more than to those in dire poverty. Indeed, the desperately poor have never belonged to any church in large numbers, save for 'Erin's root fed hordes', Irish people fleeing from famine who were Roman Catholics. The values of thrift, frugality and cleanliness – Wesley really did say 'cleanliness is next to godliness' – produced someone who 'tended to be a highly disciplined, self-controlled person, willing to train his mind in critical thinking and his voice in harmony singing'.[2]

For women – well over 50% of Methodist members were and are women – the movement provided a warm community, an alternative to the public house. Moreover, it gave the artisan group as a whole a sense of purpose and scope for office in the local community, even if the lives of the Methodists last century were limited to home, work and chapel. Methodism, in short, was a dynamic influence on the 'respectable poor' enabling some to become aspiring middle class. An example is provided by the home of Sir Herbert Butterfield (1900–1979) at Oxenhope, in Brontë Country near Haworth. Herbert's father Albert, was a woolsorter and later a clerk at the mill, where a Methodist friend, somewhat higher up the social scale, helped him. Albert set great store by the 'class meeting' (a small group gathered for spiritual fellowship), which he led for years. Young Herbert was encouraged by his father in all his aspirations; and throughout a lifetime culminating in the Regius Professorship of History and the Vice Chancellorship of Cambridge University, Sir Herbert took part in his fellowship meetings [1].

---

1. It was the land of moorland villages where the Methodist chapel was the source of society and civilization, and in that community he grew up . . . He retained the simplicity, a touch at times of the austerity and always the loyalties of his childhood . . . some things or persons he was vehemently against. The first was purveyors of panaceas especially when they are politicians, men who propose to us the way to Utopia . . . the second thing he was against was hierarchy. He kept to the end the critique, the stance of the chapel in the moors against too institutionalized a Christianity . . . It was part of an intellectual integrity so absolute that at moments it frightened.

*Source*: Sir Owen Chadwick. Memorial Service to Sir Herbert Butterfield. Great St Mary's Church, Cambridge, 13 October 1979.

The dangers of such an ethos can be smug respectability, an over-stress on combating drinking, gambling and sexual misdemeanours. The positive side was a concern about education and civic pride – the leaders of both major political parties in York in 1900 were Methodists and Salem Methodist New Connexion Chapel in Halifax was called 'The Mayors' Nest' because it provided so many Mayors to the town! There was a flow of Methodists into the great 'caring' professions as they developed, revealing very much the importance of being earnest. 'Be active,' said John Wesley, 'be diligent, avoid all laziness, sloth, indolence, flee from every degree, every appearance of it, else you will never be more than a half Christian.'

In the 1980s when Margaret Thatcher, as Prime Minister, and Michael Foot, as leader of the opposition, faced one another across the Dispatch Box in the House of Commons, they represented, as people brought up in Methodism – like it or not – the Methodist influence on society [2].

---

2. I was brought up to work jolly hard. We were taught self-respect. You were taught tremendous pride in your country. All these were Victorian values.

*Source*: Lady Thatcher, *The Standard*, April 1983.

We must fight the good fight and keep the faith. Books were weapons – the most beloved and the sharpest. And there spread before us were enemies enough for a life time; historical figures and their modern counterparts melted into one; brewers, protectionists, papists, Spanish tyrants and Stuart kings – . . . sons of Belial or Beelzebub normally disguised as West Country Tories.

*Source*: Michael Foot, *Debts of Honour*, Picador 1981, p. 13.

---

Methodism was not the dominant element in the early Labour Party, but it produced many, in both the Liberal Party and the early Labour movement, whose religious idealism fostered political idealism, thereby largely preventing in England the bitter anti-clericalism which typified continental socialism. Here [3] is Sir George Edwards MP, a typical product of the Primitive Methodist Church's great impact on the rural poor in Norfolk and Suffolk in the 1870s and 1880s.

---

3. With the study of theology I soon began to realize that the social conditions of the people were not as God intended they should be. The gross injustice meted out to my parents and the terrible suffering I had to undergo in my boyhood burnt themselves into my soul like a hot iron. Many a time did I vow that I would do something to better the condition of my class.

*Source*: Sir George Edwards, *From Crow Scaring to Westminster*, London 1922, p. 36.

---

Edwards had many precursors who found their ability to read, speak, think and debate in chapel, combining their theology often enough with radical politics, even if few actually prayed for the death of 'blacklegs' in a strike as happened at Seaton Delaval in the 1830s. The impact of Methodism on workers like the Northumberland and Durham miners is complex. Robert Moore,[3] describing the Deerness Valley, records the reply of a recent convert who was being taunted with the story of Jesus turning water into wine. 'Well, if Jesus could turn beer into clothes for his children and furniture for his house, would he not be able to turn water into wine?' The negative side was a division of working men into pub or chapel, respectable or unrespectable working class. Towards Sedgley in the Black Country, the Fighting Cocks Inn and the Methodist Church stood symbolically opposite one another.

Methodism did not save, indeed could not have saved, England from a French style revolution but it may have played a notable role in producing for a generation or two what Professor Harold Perkin called a 'viable class society', now painfully disintegrating.[4] Religion may, in fact, loom larger in early twentieth-century society than meets the eye. What else explains the stability of the 1930s at a time of intense economic pressure?

Methodism's social thinking has been basically individualist, despite the deep concern for social justice expressed in the struggle for workers' rights in mines and agricultural areas. There is also the pioneering work of Dr Thomas Bowman Stephenson in founding both the National Children's Home (now NCH Action for Children) and the Wesley Deaconess Order (now Methodist Diaconal Order). Late Victorian Methodism, led by the fiery Welshman Hugh Price Hughes, despite its occasionally naive approach to politics, pioneered a style of mission alongside – or perhaps for – the poor in great cities like Manchester, Leeds, Bristol, Birmingham and innerbelt and central London. This was an attempt to grapple with the casualties of the 'Two Nations' of Victorian England, so linking with the modest enterprises of our day.

Today we still maintain a link with the past by fostering mission at home and overseas.

## 2.  A sense of world mission

I once asked a lady who had joined our church 'out of the blue', 'What has it meant for you?' 'Oh,' she said, 'You have plugged me into a wider world. I never knew about the Overseas Church, the National Children's Home, Mission Alongside the Poor and all that. Here's a box for NCH. Help me next Saturday with our street collection.' And I did! When children come round for JMA (Junior Mission for All), remember that it goes back to the beginning of Methodism. When John Wesley wrote to a friend who had criticized him for preaching in other clergymen's parishes, 'I look upon all the world as my parish', he was using a phrase which was characteristic of the Evangelical Revival which, having begun in Europe, spread to America and Great Britain. The idea of World Mission was fostered in Methodism by Thomas Coke, who died on the way to India. He was a visionary, but an organizer like Jabez Bunting (1779–1858) was needed to make the vision viable. The whole enterprise was a sign of the sheer energy available in Georgian and Regency England. Later ventures in mission coincided with the expansion of power in the Second British Empire and with developments like the nineteenth-century 'Scramble for Africa' by the European powers.

In Methodism, there was also a concern about slavery and a wide sense of responsibility which sometimes found expression in an unfortunate tone. Sir William McArthur, for example, pleaded with Gladstone's government for the annexation of the Fiji Islands, only to draw a retort in parliament that there was undue concern lest '2,000 ferocious mountaineers should eat up 150,000 Methodists'. Support for the concept of the British Empire now seems very strange to us, but it remained part of the 'mind set' of many until after the Second World War. There was also a genuine trusteeship principle towards colonial peoples which, in the end, fuelled much of the impetus to independence. Nationalist leaders, after all, were often trained in mission schools.

Each Methodist is automatically a member of the Missionary Society. The visit of the 'Missionary' on furlough in Victorian and later days enabled many a village Methodist to realize a sense of world parish, when it was so easy to make one's parish one's world. Now we can hardly be unaware of the 'global village' and its needs, especially when so many of us travel overseas. We live in a multi-racial and multi-cultural society. Our stress is now on *partnership* and Great Britain is a mission field [4].

4. The Conference affirmed that the place of British Methodism within the world-wide Church involves the privilege and duty of welcoming Christians from overseas to work in Britain and of offering personnel to the Church overseas . . .

The Conference recorded its thanks for the £2,838,239 raised in the home Districts for general funds and £62,926 for Second Mile Projects.

*Source*: *Minutes of the Methodist Conference*, 1995, p. 3.

## 3.  The Methodist Churches in 1932

Now we go back to the churches which, stemming from Wesleyan and later revivals, came together in

1932 after quite prolonged negotiations, begun during the First World War.

Firstly, there was the Wesleyan Methodist Church which arose directly from the work of John Wesley. It had 517,551 members, 2,510 ministers, 18,785 local preachers, 770,716 Sunday school children and 8,152 chapels. In constituency, as we have seen, it was largely lower middle class and middle class with heavy representation among growing professional groups, such as teachers and local government clerks and artisan groups, such as skilled engineers. This was especially so in the North. The strength of the church lay in the large northern towns, in Lincolnshire, around Bristol, in the South West, and the London suburbs through migration of population, with strong Central Halls in cities such as Manchester, Liverpool, Leeds, Sheffield, Bolton and Birmingham, though the role of these institutions was changing.

Secondly, there was the Primitive Methodist Church, which originated in the Potteries and Cheshire Plain revivals of the early nineteenth century and spread across the Midlands into East Anglia and northwards up into the East Riding of Yorkshire and the coalfields of Durham and Northumberland. It was at first largely rural, then grew in industrial villages – hence its popularity among miners, fisherfolk, agricultural labourers and the nailers of the Black Country. By 1932 it had become rather more middle class than in the early days but was strong still among the working class in its heartland, especially in the North East. Primitive Methodism brought into the wider union men and women who combined a genuine piety of a simple Quaker-like style with a concern for social righteousness and social justice. Typical was Jim Simmons of Brierley Hill, a member of Attlee's Labour government of 1945, who espoused Primitive Methodism, teetotalism and an idealistic brand of socialism which clearly owed much more to Methodism than to Marx. Into union, Primitive Methodism brought 222,021 members, (including African members), 1,131 ministers, 12,896 local preachers, 277,792 Sunday school children and 4,356 buildings.

Thirdly, there was the United Methodist Church,

itself an amalgamation in 1907 of three quite distinct groups. The Methodist New Connexion, which broke away from the Wesleyans in 1797, stressed the need for a more democratic conference. The Bible Christians, who were largely to be found in the South West, along the south coast and the Isle of Wight, paralleled the Primitive Methodists after 1815. The United Methodist Free Churches of 1857 brought together groups which could not stomach the authoritarian style of Wesleyanism, in which Conference was solely ministerial until 1878. For the strong laymen of Yorkshire and Lancashire wanted to be both captains of industry and controllers of the chapels. The United Methodists were strongest in the north, especially in Yorkshire and Lancashire, the centre of the disruptions of the 1830s and 1840s typified by chapels like Baillie Street, Rochdale and George Street, Burton upon Trent. They were in some ways like strong Congregationalist pastorates with long ministerial periods of residence. There were 179,551 members, 729 ministers, 5,232 local preachers, 223,395 Sunday school children and 2,900 chapels. The constituency was solidly lower middle class and petit bourgeois, by and large higher up the social scale than the Primitives. In towns like Halifax, where prominent laymen like Mackintosh, the toffee manufacturer – 'Quality Street', indeed – were influential, there was almost an 'aristocracy of United Methodism', paralleled by the position of Sir William Hartley, the jam manufacturer, in Primitive Methodism, and Joseph Rank (1854–1943), the flour miller and T. R. Ferens (1847–1930) in Wesleyanism. They were men who knew that 'religion, self-discipline, temperance and hard work had been good for them and they sought to employ whatever means they could, in their homes, Sunday Schools, chapels, businesses and communities, to persuade, exhort and even oblige others to live by the same lights'.[5]

## For discussion

1. Think about your family history. Does anything in the analysis ring bells with you?
2. In your church do they still talk about being 'Wesleyan' or 'Primitive'? Does it matter now at all?

3. Examine the class structure of your church. Why do you think it is what it is? Are there more women than men? Why?

4. Are people's political views today in any way motivated by their religious beliefs?

5. Was that lady representative when she said she was 'plugged into a wider world'? Does the church do that for people? If not, why not?

6. Is there a real concern for the poor in your church? How would you define 'poor'?

# 2

# Methodism 1932–1950

## 1. Methodist Union

The church does not live in a world apart from the rest of humanity. The First World War revealed the great gap between many people and the churches. The late 1920s and early 1930s saw the effect of economic depression with widespread unemployment and deprivation and, at the same time, a stability which may have owed much to Victorian values and the 'folk religion' of the Sunday School.

Less than six months after the Duke and Duchess of York (later King George VI and Queen Elizabeth) had witnessed the inauguration of the Methodist Church at the Albert Hall by the signing of the Deed of Union on 20 September 1932, Adolf Hitler became Chancellor of the Third Reich in Berlin. There was consequent tension in the churches (and not least in Methodism) between the pacifists and 'pacificists' (a preferable word to 'appeasers'), who wanted at all costs to avoid another European war, and the realists, who began to support re-armament, with thinkers like Reinhold Niebuhr exercising increasing influence on leaders like the Archbishop of York, William Temple. The national government, led by Ramsay Macdonald and Stanley Baldwin, had taken office in 1931 at a time when unemployment reached three million. Christian leaders backed the League of Nations and the concept of collective security, while at the same time supporting disarmament. There was still a sense of guilt that the provisions of the Treaty of Versailles (1919), which bore fruit in due time in the failure of the Weimar Republic and the rise of Nazism, had been grossly unfair. In Italy the Fascist Duce (Benito Mussolini) and the Pope (Pius XI) had reached agreement, the Lateran Treaty of 1929 guaranteeing certain rights to the Roman Catholic Church in Italy and confirming the Vatican as a state. Indeed, a corporate style of national state was not uncongenial to some elements in Roman Catholicism at the time. We must not exaggerate resistance to the fascist dictators.

This is the background against which we must analyse the Methodism of the 1930s while avoiding the hindsight of knowing that within seven years the Second World War would change the style of the Methodist Church and other communions. The negotiations leading to union, beginning in earnest in 1918, were not easy but were helped by the growing similarity of the three churches both in social constituency and in style, though the United Methodists and Primitive Methodists made no bones about their nonconformity and their espousal of the rights of the laity. Constitutional compromise was reached reasonably easily. The Legal Hundred – the hundred ministers who had to ratify any resolution of the Wesleyan Conference – would disappear, being replaced by 'Conference elected representatives', ministers and lay people appointed by Conference for a limited period who thus provided some continuity.

The keenest debate was over the role, and indeed continuance, of the 'ministerial' or 'pastoral' session of the Conference which in Wesleyan Methodism dealt particularly with the training, stationing and disciplining of the ministers. In the end this arrangement was accepted by the more liberal group and has remained, despite some determined attempts to get rid of it. It provides a link with the itinerant preachers of Wesley's time, giving the feel of an 'order' not unlike some of the monastic orders or the Dominican Order of Friars. It was agreed that the President of Conference should be an ordained minister and the Vice-President a lay person, each holding office for a year. The idea of annual Presidents goes back to the time after 'Wesley's death when it was agreed that there were to be 'no more kings in Israel'. Several Presidents since union had been president of their churches prior to Union, but since Union only Dr Donald English has been elected twice – in 1978 and 1990. The first woman President, Dr Kathleen Richardson, was elected in 1992. Thirteen women Vice-Presidents have followed Mrs Mildred Lewis, elected in 1948. It must be remembered that women were not ordained to the presbyteral ministry until 1974. Annual appointments make it difficult for 'the media', who at one time appeared to think that Lord Soper was perpetual President.

The principal difficulties in the union negotiations were doctrinal. On the surface the Wesleyans had a 'higher' view of the ordained ministry than the Primitive and United Methodists, but the hierarchical view of the ministry had effectively broken down in 1878 when lay people were admitted to the Wesleyan Conference. The Wesleyans had issued a report on *The Nature of the Church* in 1908, largely written by G. G. Findlay. A. S. Peake, the leading Primitive Methodist lay biblical scholar, seized on this statement as setting out his own view of the ordained ministry [5].

This kind of argument pulled the rug from under the feet of the 'high Wesleyans' led by Dr J. Ernest Rattenbury (1870–1963), who could no longer state the older Wesleyan view of the prerogatives of the pastoral office. A sticking point was the presiding of lay people at Holy Communion. The Wesleyans had never permitted this. For some of the others a ministerial monopoly seemed contrary to the doctrine of the priesthood of all believers, often interpreted in an individual manner. The final compromise was that laypersons might preside in a circuit if there was

---

5. Apart from the church the ministry is nothing at all. It possesses significance only as it serves the church and enables it to function more effectively. The ministry has nothing which the whole body does not possess, though functions which belong to the church as a whole may be fitly exercised by a special order . . . The minister must have his own individual call from God. But the commission to exercise his office must come to him through the Church . . . his vocation must be tested and proved by the Church. He is called to be a prophet and a priest. But the ministry has a prophetic and priestly character only because the Church already possesses it.

. . . when I heard it explained in the early days of the Union Committee that the Wesleyans did not regard their ministers as 'the paid agents of the Church', I asked myself in amazement what Methodist people entertained so grovelling a view of the ministry . . . [It is] the highest calling open to a man, the most sacred vocation, one not to be taken save on the warrant of a Divine call authenticated by the call of the Church . . . Be it ours to have a high doctrine of the ministry just because we have a high doctrine of the Church, to regard the ministry not as possessed of any priesthood which it does not share with the laity, but to recognize that priesthood finds its fittest organ and most intense expression in the activities of those who are wholly dedicated to its service.

*Sources*: A. S. Peake, 'Pray for the Peace of Jerusalem', Presidential Address to the Free Church Council, 1928, reprinted in J. T. Wilkinson (ed), *Essays in Commemoration of A. S. Peake*, Epworth Press 1958, p. 149; A. S. Peake, 'Methodist Union Opposition' in *Primitive Methodist Leader*, 8 June 1922.

---

evidence of deprivation. This principle, by and large, has prevailed for the last sixty years, along with the encouragement now of bread and wine being taken by lay people to other lay people after a service of Holy Communion, a custom long established in other churches and clearly described by Justin Martyr in 150 CE.

Wesleyans insisted on a statement on the authority of Methodism being inserted in the doctrinal clauses of the Deed of Union, though some of the phrases are rather vague and ill defined [6].

6. The Methodist Church claims and cherishes its place in the Holy Catholic Church which is the Body of Christ. It rejoices in the inheritance of the apostolic faith and loyally accepts the fundamental principles of the historic creeds and of the Protestant Reformation. It ever remembers that in the providence of God Methodism was raised up to spread scriptural holiness throughout the land by the proclamation of the evangelical faith and declares its unfaltering resolve to be true to its divinely appointed mission.

Source: *Constitutional Practice and Discipline of the Methodist Church*, Volume 2, 1993, p. 212.

In 1932 Dr Scott Lidgett defined the principles of the Reformation as 'justification by faith, the completeness and all sufficiency of our Lord's sacrifice and priesthood, the direct access of all believers to God through Him, expressed as the priesthood of all believers'.[1] This was later officially stated in the *Senior Catechism* of 1952 [7].

7. Those churches are called Protestant which have been raised up by God to revive the witness to the supreme authority of the scriptures, salvation by faith, the priesthood of all believers and the ministry of the whole church.

Source: *The Senior Catechism of the Methodist Church*, Methodist Publishing House 1952, p. 12.

The arguments for union were stated clearly and strongly by Peake and Lidgett. Indeed they both consistently looked to the corporate union not only of Methodism but of Christendom. Peake saw union as the will of God according to the New Testament. He went on to see Methodist Union as a first step because Methodists were at one at the deepest level. Thirdly, the taunts of the 'outsider' were justified if the churches remained disunited. (Sociologists are not convinced by that argument but it is consistent with the New Testament.) Fourthly, evangelism would be given new impetus. Sir Robert Perks (1846–1934) and Aldom French (1868–1962) foresaw new chapels in village areas leading to a recapture of the religious and political 'clout' of the Free Churches. Fifthly, union was in harmony with tendencies towards centralization across society including the League of Nations and monopolies in industry. The *Methodist Recorder*, which soon became the only Methodist newspaper after Union, had stated as early as 1919 'Christian unity is their definite charge from God as the League of Nations is the definite charge for the nations.' The example of the Church of Scotland (1929) was a parallel with union negotiations in Methodism. Similar problems of surplus buildings emerged.

Union itself presented few difficulties in the higher echelons of the church. The leaders were not dissimilar in style and each church had a basically parallel 'connexional' system. A good example of what became possible is found in the Temperance and Social Welfare Department, which had as its leaders for a decade Henry Carter (1874–1951), a Wesleyan, and Clifford Urwin (1884–1978), a United Methodist. Urwin was no mean political thinker and a first-class communicator. Carter, though at first embroiled in the teetotal issue, was a church leader who was aware earlier than most of the needs of refugees from Nazism. He was a pioneer of what later became the Inter-Church Aid and Refugee Service and in Britain Christian Aid. The theological colleges also quickly amalgamated. The Primitive Methodist College at Manchester, named Hartley College since 1907, joined with Victoria Park, the United Methodist College. The Wesleyan College, Didsbury also in Manchester, transferred to Bristol after World War Two. Richmond College in London, Wesley College in Leeds (which had re-opened in 1930), Handsworth College in Birmingham, and Wesley House at Cambridge continued, as did the Wesleyan Colleges of Education, Westminster College for men in London (after World War Two, at Oxford) and Southlands College, Wimbledon, for women (now part of the Roehampton Institute). (Both Colleges of Education later accepted students of both sexes.) To the Wesleyan public schools were added United Methodism's Ashville College, Harrogate and the two Bible Christian foundations in the South West, Shebbear College and Edgehill College for Girls.

The great hopes for union were not fulfilled. Reality was very different from the dreams of Peake and Perks. Church people – and Methodists are no exception – tend to be 'local' rather than 'cosmopolitan', to use the sociological terms. 'Local' people feel an enormous sense of belonging to their particular chapel, often due to deep family ties. Chapel – its life, its ethos, its people – could not easily be let go, and consequently closures pointed to non-viability rather than to great enthusiasm for union. Here is a somewhat cynical assessment of the situation [8].

8. Unionists were caught in a peculiar dilemma. On the one hand if union was to make Methodism a greater evangelistic force throughout the country, the rationalization consequent upon closure of overlapping chapels was essential. On the other hand if they advocated closure of chapels as the main plank of their programme, the union movement was doomed. They prevaricated . . . the purpose of union was to close the chapels, the price of union was to keep them open.

*Source*: R. Currie, *Methodism Divided*, Faber & Faber 1968, pp. 197–98.

That is a harsh judgment, but union was a merger without the toughness to be found in commercial and industrial amalgamations. Circuits often remained static or were simply enlarged. A former United Methodist, William Gowland, when a probationer minister at Port Erin on the Isle of Man, found rival shopkeepers of Wesleyan and Primitive Methodist origin retaining their rival chapels as well as their shops! In Burton upon Trent the United Methodist Circuit (the strongest) remained intact, the Wesleyans and Primitive Methodists united, and the three only finally combined well after the Second World War in the Trinity circuit. Even then a smaller Primitive Methodist circuit, with one town chapel sandwiched between two others in the Trinity circuit, remained independent and produced a circuit 'Sabbath Plan' on which the preachers were numbered rather than

named. On the other hand, in suburban Wolverhampton, Beckminster church, built in 1926 at the same time as a large suburban and council house area, drew to itself lay leaders from all the constituent churches. Consequently I knew nothing as a boy of 'Prims' or 'Wesleyans' and all that! Far different was a mining community in South Derbyshire which had three large chapels, all with a strong communal and worshipping life. In 1962 they still required six preachers each Sunday; by 1995 only two of the chapels remained, representing rather different styles of churchmanship.

This failure faced Methodism with a cruel dilemma. In the 1950s 'redundancy' had become a scandal, especially for younger ministers who felt their time was squandered in duplicating unnecessary meetings. Immediately after union there were 1,362 circuits in England, Wales and Scotland, and 115 amalgamations took place before 1939. During that period the sale of 209 chapels out of 14,341 was authorized, while 321 new chapels were built, many to replace older buildings. Dr Eric Baker, Secretary of Conference in the 1950s, said that the sequel of Methodist union challenged the assumption that the unification of ministers and central departments will ever be sufficient to guarantee effective union where it really matters – that is, where the Christian meets the non-Christian. Baker added in 1959: 'We have far too many churches, many of which were erected before the present age of easy transport brought about a situation where fewer and better churches are among the first requirements.' Many in positions of leadership and ministers 'at the bottom' agreed with Baker. Some of the chapels closed, but sadly left great gaps in the innerbelt areas of cities and towns, for it was often the weakest that went to the wall. In the northern end of one Midland town six chapels closed in the twenty years after 1962. No blame is cast, but such was the legacy of lack of radical strategic planning. At local level, it soon became obvious that Methodist union had offered no really new ideas about church organization, but simply provided an uneasy compromise which yielded little experimentation.

It must be admitted that the churches brought to union an ageing leadership. The first President, John Scott Lidgett (1854–1953), was a theologian and church leader of the very highest order with wide interests in education and politics. But he was seventy-eight, and was followed by Luke Wiseman (1858–1944), a distinguished missioner and musician also well into his seventies. The first Vice-President, Sir Robert Perks, was in his eighties. All these men and most of their successors – W. C. Jackson was one exception – were well beyond the peak of intellectual agility. Lidgett and Wiseman were still active during the war, with Lidgett involved in the Education Act of 1944 and only ceasing to be 'Chairman' of a district in 1948. He preached at the World Methodist Ecumenical Conference in 1951 at St Mary's, Oxford. As Adrian Hastings pungently put it, 'Methodism had arrived. Was it also about to pass away?'[2] It is only fair to point out that the age of church leaders was paralleled in the Church of England with Cosmo Gordon Lang (1864–1945) who became Archbishop of Canterbury at sixty-five, following the octogenarian Davidson (1848–1930). William Temple, as Archbishop of York, represented a new generation. Even Henry Carter, perhaps the liveliest figure of comparable age in Methodism, had been in connexional office as Temperance and Social Welfare Secretary in Wesleyanism since 1911.

The Methodist Church in 1932 organized itself on highly traditional lines [9]. Conference was the supreme governing body – the corporate bishop – with approximately 600 (now 384) ministerial and lay representatives. There was a powerful General Purposes Committee and Departments (as they were called before the change to Divisions in 1974), located, with the exception of the Manchester-based Chapel Department, in London. At district level the Synods, which mirrored Conference, had lay representatives elected by the circuits and were presided over by a minister known as the 'Chairman of the District', an office going back to 1791. Initially he had other duties, usually as a Superintendent Minister in his district, but later, after the 1939–45 war, he was 'separated' to be pastor of the pastors and district

missioner. The circuit had its Superintendent Minister, who had enormous episcopal power if he cared to use it. He presided at the circuit Quarterly Meeting, which goes back to 1748, and at the other necessary circuit committees matching those at connexional level.

---

9. *The 1932–1974 Constitution*

A: Organs of consultation and decision:

*At national level*:
The Conference, meeting in two sessions:
– the Representative session
– the Ministerial session

General Purposes Committee

*At District level*:
The Synod, meeting in two sessions:
– the Representative session
– the Ministerial session

*At Circuit level*:
the Circuit Quarterly Meeting

*At local church level*:
– the Trustees' meeting
– the Leaders' meeting
– the Society Meeting (i.e. meeting of all Members)

B: Organs of connexional administration:

*The Departments*

Methodist Missionary Society
Home Mission Department (London Mission)
Department of Connexional Funds
Department of Chapel Affairs
Sunday School and Education Departments (after 1943, Youth Department)
Temperance and Social Welfare Department (after 1950, Christian Citizenship Department)
Ministerial Training Department
Local Preachers Department
Methodist Publishing House and Epworth Press

*Source*: For basic facts and a useful commentary, F. Baker, *A Charge to Keep*, Epworth Press 1954, pp. 182ff.

In the local church (or 'society', to use the original Methodist term) there were two key meetings. The Trustees, who were responsible for the chapel and ancillary premises, were sometimes men of property themselves. Women trustees were rare, but became more common after the war, humanizing what could be a rather formal business meeting. The Leaders' Meeting would concern itself with all the manifold activities of the church. Finance was divided between 'trust' (i.e. property costs) and 'society' (i.e. maintenance of church life), with the 'Society Fund' being the sum out of which the circuit would receive the 'assessment' to pay the ministers, to maintain their houses ('manses') and to pay district and 'connexional' dues such as those for training ministers and running the 'Departments'. When trustees became rather remote from a younger generation, clashes could occur! Other bodies in the church had their own committee structure. In the north, for example, Sunday Schools have a measure of autonomy stemming from their role in Victorian England.

## 2. At the grass roots

At this time, then, Methodism had a leadership of a liberal evangelical stance with a flash of the old fervour and a concern for the life of the community and nation. But what of the grass roots? Two Methodist churches in the Midlands provide relevant evidence. The first, Grainger's Lane, Cradley Heath, is Primitive Methodist and owes its existence to a revival among the nailmakers – their trade is typical of the Black Country – in the last century. The building, dating from 1906, is mock gothic, and the gowned minister and choir represent a style of worship and preaching difficult to envisage in the days when a Christian 'nailer', the only man in 'the shop' who could read, read the newspaper to his mates at work.[3]

This church and its ministers developed an educational style which seems to be a blend of the Workers' Educational Association, the modern 'university of the third age' and an attempt to pass on a distinctive Christian inheritance to a new generation very differ-

ent from the days of Camp Meetings. Dr Alan Wilkinson depicts his father's endeavours to enable the congregation to enter into the great literary, artistic and theological riches of the pre-1914 world in which he was nurtured.[4] In 1932 Grainger's Lane had 700 Sunday School children, with 200 church members, though 700 sometimes attended Sunday evening worship. This was typical of the dissent of the period. There were many more 'adherents' than members. That large penumbra of worshippers has subsequently disappeared. Apart from Sunday School and evening worship there was morning worship, four classes for young people on Sunday afternoons, Women's Own on Monday afternoons, Band of Hope and Junior Christian Endeavour on Monday evening, and preaching service on Tuesday evening. (In some areas the midweek preaching service lingered into the 1950s.) Senior Christian Endeavour (CE) and Sunday School preparation groups met on Wednesday with Intermediate CE on Thursday, and Sister's class with Young People's Educational Association on Friday. All this, in Wilkinson's words, was 'mind expanding and character building'. Missionary work was stressed. Citizenship tended to emphasize Sunday observance, temperance and the evils of gambling, the typical Methodist pietism of the day. For the person with local church loyalties this was a church life of great intensity, the 'institutional church' which was a product of late Victorian social change.

We now move a few miles to suburban Wolverhampton. Here is Beckminster, built in 1926 by Crouch, Butler and Savage who were architects of several churches in the gothic style in the West Midlands. A bishop, noting the chancel and side pulpit, quipped: 'The most Anglican church in Wolverhampton'. Worship was twice a Sunday. In the 1940s the evening service was still the best attended with a real 'buzz' of evangelical fervour, though never fundamentalist. Sunday School in the afternoon was fully 'graded' according to the approach which became the norm at the time, with a fine team of teachers. Many who went through that Sunday School went on to become leaders in church and community. The Bible was central but taught in a relaxed modern style. We gained a knowledge of the framework of the biblical story on which we could build without having to unlearn pious nonsense. Responsive worship was frequent, though I recall boredom at extempore prayer! The mid-week programmes included a strong Wesley Guild with its four-fold shape of consecration, culture, Christian service and comradeship, and our minister (Arthur N. Rose) wrote the devotions in the Connexional Guild magazine. It is not always realized how many young people learned to pray and preside and speak at Wesley Guild or Christian Endeavour; Lord Tonypandy, Speaker of the House of Commons in the 1970s, was one, learning to speak at Tonypandy Guild, with 'shaking hands'. New fellowship groups for men and women became the heart of this church, participating fellowship in contrast to the older 'educational' style at Grainger's Lane. A new generation could get that elsewhere. The fellowships catered for all tastes including, during the war, a Padre's Hour for soldiers at the local anti-aircraft battery. This survives into the 1990s. The youth club, begun in 1943, anticipated the creation of the National Association of Youth Clubs, which features in a later chapter. A full range of uniformed organizations completed a full catering for youth. Later a Day Centre for the elderly and handicapped reflected a changing neighbourhood.

Sociologically, this church was middle class or lower middle class with a large number of teachers of all ages. Successive ministers brought all-round skills of a high order. The role of the minister was clear – pastor, preacher, leader of worship, trainer of members in groups or residential conferences, fosterer of vocation. The general administration and finance was in the hands of capable lay leaders. This was an infectious congregation, a model of what a suburban congregation could be. Many young people, coming into this church from families right outside the church, were trained for Christian discipleship and church membership. This combined a distinctively Methodist ethos with a liberal-evangelical style which was much more open to wider culture than either older dissenting styles of evangelicalism or a fundamentalist type which tends in a strange way to use the technology of modern culture to foster what is in danger of becoming a religious ghetto.

There were many other styles of Methodist church life in this period. Let us go to Crockleford in Suffolk. The Methodist chapel is the only building in the hamlet. Sunday morning and afternoon is worship time with a small Sunday School using the *Golden Bells* hymnbook. The communion service is non-responsive, since this is a chapel still very much in the Primitive Methodist tradition. The organist is flanked at worship – as she was when I was minister there in the 1950s – by two brothers – farmers, one of whom plays the violin, the other a viola. There is a Women's Fellowship and a fortnightly Bible study, led by the minister, which alternates with a prayer meeting. The group will take the best the minister can offer. The church has a keen sense of support for Overseas Missions and for the London Mission. The contrast with Grainger's Lane or Beckminster or Westminster Central Hall is immense, but the Methodist characteristics are equally valid. There are many more Crocklefords than Beckminsters! Forty per cent of Methodist churches in 1995 had under twenty-eight members.

## 3. Social thinking and spirituality

The 1930s saw few great changes in the church, though the world – thanks to movements in culture as well as the menace of Hitler – was changing rapidly. This was the heyday of the cinema – Anna Neagle, Fred Astaire, Mickey Mouse and Snow White – and Disney was king. Many went to 'the pictures' each week. It was the age of radio too. G. Bramwell Evens, from 1929 to 1939 the minister of King Cross Methodist Church, Halifax, was 'Romany' to hundreds of thousands of children as he gave word pictures of the world of nature. Later the voice of C. S. Lewis, and Dorothy L. Sayers' *The Man Born to be King* (1943) would, for some, bring the story of the Gospels alive as never before. Radio, too, enabled worship styles to become familiar across the denominations. Methodists like Professor John Foster, Frederic Greeves, Kenneth Grayston, Leslie Weatherhead,

Gordon Rupp and Donald Soper (off air during the war as a pacifist) became familiar 'wireless' speakers.

Christian citizenship became an increasing concern in Methodism. Here [10] are the aims of Henry Carter's department.

---

10. *The Responsibility of the Department of Christian Citizenship* shall be the presentation of the Christian social witness. The subject within its purview in addition to the Temperance movement shall embrace social questions including industrial welfare, gambling, public health and social purity, the Christian observance of Sunday, world peace, international relationships, the preparation for and practice of Christian citizenship and the maintenance of the Christian ideal in social life. The Department is authorized to take action in respect of the public affairs specified in the foregoing paragraph in harmony with the existing declarations or resolutions of the Conference.

*Source*: *Minutes of Conference*, 1933, repeated yearly, later amended.

---

The difficulty is that unless other churches, and especially the Church of England, agree on concerted action, the Methodist Church does not possess sufficient political 'clout', and appears isolated and self-absorbed. It is easy, too, to caricature the late Victorian and early twentieth-century concern of Methodism with what was called the 'drink evil' and 'the sin of gambling'. Carter had become the Methodist expert in this field. His slogan 'elevate, educate, legislate' was always in terms of persuasion rather than prohibition. This made for an uneasy relationship with the United Kingdom Alliance which clearly favoured prohibition, as indeed did the Wesleyan Conference. Carter was a member of the Royal Commission on Licensing which reported in 1932. The recommendations were hardly radical. The legislative legacy was almost nil.

The united church made its views about drink and gambling crystal clear. As late as 1951 Conference re-affirmed the 1933 statement on *Total Abstinence and Temperance Reform*, re-iterating the call to abstain from intoxicating liquors as beverages but making clear that total abstinence was not a condition of church membership. Alcohol 'assails the highest centres of personality, it impairs conscience, judgment and the sense of responsibility'. Example, therefore, is vital. 'The use of intoxicants on Methodist premises is not permitted.' 'Methodists should keep themselves free from complicity with a traffic the results of which are so injurious to the interests of religion, morality and social life.' Temperance teaching should be given 'in all youth organizations associated with the Methodist church with a systematic enrolment of total abstainers'. One might ask if this stance made barriers between Methodism and the working class. By 1975 the mood had changed. It was recognized that many Methodists were no longer abstainers. Paradoxically, the problem of alcohol is more prominent now than it was in 1932, and it is now seen as part of a complex drug problem.

Gambling, defined clearly in 1936 [11], is seen as contrary to an acceptance of a divine will and providence. Belief in luck cannot be reconciled with faith in God. Certainly Methodism should not resort to gambling or allow any form of it on its premises. It is in fact 'a sin'. Conference wished for the abolition of the 'totalisator' and for the exclusion of any form of gambling from the press – as in public libraries! – and the ultimate elimination of the 'bookmaker' and any form of gambling for revenue purposes. In 1933 Benson Perkins (1881–1974) became chairman of The Churches' Committee on Gambling. Did it have, we may wonder, a rather paternalist concern for working people in danger of squandering 'dole money', paralleled in 1994 by references to the National Lottery as a 'tax on the poor'? Perkins clashed with the Anglican moral theologian R. C. Mortimer who saw no harm in 'surplus money' being spent on frivolity. This illustrates the point about Methodism's isolation, as does the horror of Dr Eric Baker (1899–1973) in 1959 when he asked some young people to draw a picture illustrating Methodism. A girl drew a wine glass crossed out! Carter's 'Young Abstainers' League had ambivalent consequences.

11. By gambling those practices are meant whose characteristic features are a) determination of the possession of money or value by an appeal to chance, b) the gains of the winners are made at the expense of the losers, c) gain is secured without rendering in service or in value equivalent to the gain obtained. Gambling takes the following forms – gaming or playing for money in a game of chance, betting or staking money on a doubtful or uncertain event, lotteries and sweepstakes which may be defined as the distribution of prizes by lot or chance, gambling speculation in the realm of finance and commerce . . . based upon the fluctuations of market prices and in essence consists of an attempt to gain through the loss of other people without rendering any commensurate service.

*Source*: *Declarations of Conference on Social Questions*, 1959, p. 50.

The problem of alcohol and the lure of the lottery are still with us on a growing scale. A Methodist contribution of note – much more positive than the older style which, despite the notable work among alcoholics at Kingsway Hall and other missions, could be alienating – was the work of Gordon Moody (1912–1994). He pioneered group therapy and counselling, typified by Gamblers Anonymous, and became a spokesman for the churches who never patronized his hearers. In 1992 minor gambling was allowed on Methodist premises. No longer have ministers to agonize over 'guessing the name of the cat'. Recent statements like *The Non-Medical use of Drugs* (1974), *Through a Glass Darkly – Responsible Attitudes to Alcohol* (1987) and *The Winners Shout, The Losers Curse* (1989) are much more positive, less moralizing. Ironically, the National Lottery has brought the gambling issue sharply to the foreground. Conference condemned it in 1995, other churches have followed. Could the changes in Methodist statements on these issues be an example of what Dr Edward Norman claims to be characteristic of Christian ethical statements – that they tend to follow secular patterns a decade or so later? Or was the shift a part of the continued development of a 'society' into a 'church'?

Other statements of the pre-war period include the *Significance and Use of Leisure* (1935, revised 1974) and the *Christian Observance of Sunday* (1939, revised 1973). 'Christian households', we are told, 'will be very careful before they admit cricket or tennis or golf or billiards or cards into the Sunday programme', but cultural interests will not be discouraged. In other words, books, music, art and 'such occupations as develop the mind' are fine – Bach but not bowls! Entertainment on Sunday is discouraged and 'the modern habit of using the car to visit friends or to travel to the country on Sunday may be the cause of a perilous weakening of family life . . . there is abundant evidence that a Sunday of which a large part is spent at services in school or chapel may be the happiest and most profitable day of the week. Moreover there is every reason why the family should sit together at public worship wherever possible.' The due observance of Sunday, in short, is essential to the Christian life. One wonders, in fact, how the early church survived before Constantine.

Thanks to the lack of new ideas, the ethos of Methodism in the 1930s was rather monochrome, though younger scholars and thinkers were emerging. Some were searching for greater depth in spirituality. New movements in Methodism characteristically take the form of fellowships, which do not harden into exclusive 'parties', and the circuit system can effectively prevent the dominance of any one grouping. This has drawbacks as well as advantages. Methodist ministers accommodate themselves to various pastoral situations without becoming ecclesiastical chameleons. The Fellowship of the Kingdom (FK) provided a meeting place for ministers who wished to explore religious experience and the Bible. The dominant mood was typified by the Baptist classical scholar T. R. Glover's *The Jesus of History* (1917) and in Methodism by the biblical scholarship of Alexander Findlay (1880–1961) of Didsbury College, Manchester, whose influence was pervasive. In many chapels the preaching presupposed a theology in which Jesus was Master and Friend as well as Saviour and Lord. This was certainly the emphasis at Beckminster, Wolverhampton during and after the war, when Mortimer Sinfield (1900–1989) combined in his preaching the biblical insight of his tutor Findlay with the homiletical style of W. E. Sangster.

Russell Maltby (1866–1950), Warden of the Wesley Deaconess Order, was another significant figure in renewal. William Temple thought him unsurpassed in his appeal to students. Theological leadership was given by elder statesmen like Herbert B. Workman, the historian of monasticism, biographer of Wyclif, and Principal of Westminster College. R. Newton Flew (1888–1962), of Wesley House, Cambridge, soon became one of the most influential ecumenical leaders in the area of Faith and Order. The publications of the Fellowship of the Kingdom and the parallel School of Fellowship, which included lay people, were very significant and typical of the best thinking of the period. Here Methodist ministers exercised the role of middle-men between the scholars and the pew.

Some, like John Hunter and W. E. Orchard in Congregationalism, sought deeper spirituality and richer corporate worship, related to more frequent sacramental observance. Orchard, in the end, became a Roman Catholic, and there were a few Methodists, of whom T. S. Gregory is the best known, who moved in the same direction. To Gregory, the historian Christopher Hill [12], brought up a Methodist, dedicated one of his books:

---

12. The dedication acknowledges a thirty five year old debt which can never be repaid. How can one ever be sufficiently grateful to the person who first showed one that all accepted truths, just because they are accepted, tend to become lies.

Source: C. Hill, *Intellectual Origins of the English Revolution*, OUP 1965, Preface.

---

The Methodist Sacramental Fellowship, founded in 1935, sought a richer form of prayer and worship, expressed a more traditional credal theology, and evoked the quest for corporate reunion. The defection of Gregory led to cries of 'popery'. Dr Henry Bett of Handsworth College felt that the holy communion was being isolated from other means of grace, but A. E. Whitham and J. E. Rattenbury were able to show that the Fellowship was loyally Methodist, with its long inheritance in styles of corporate prayer. Rattenbury combined sacramentalism with a passion for evangelism which, though varied in style, was never far below the surface in any of the Methodist groups. A stream of books from Rattenbury, which included his notable studies of the Wesley hymns, illustrates this mood. He was not out of sympathy with another stream of rather more revivalist theology, combined with Catholic sympathies, in Samuel Chadwick. Chadwick died in 1932, but his influence lived on in Cliff College in Derbyshire. Its evangelists, known as 'trekkers', conducted missions in an almost Franciscan style and its training of lay teachers and prospective ministers maintained links with the holiness tradition, especially in the Southport Convention.

The somewhat 'Catholic' phase associated with the 'Wesley-Catholics' was followed, as in Congregationalism, by a renewal of the Reformation tradition. J. S. Whale, Nathaniel Micklem, Principal of Mansfield College, Oxford, and Bernard Manning saw in the Reformed tradition a style of sacramentalism which had been downplayed in liberal Nonconformity. Manning sought to recall Methodism to the spiritual and theological riches in the Wesley hymns, and the support of Henry Bett and Newton Flew led, in some quarters, to a resurgence of the use of the Wesley corpus. As a result, many in the 1940s developed a love for an inheritance now almost buried in what Bett would have denounced as the products of 'second rate poetasters'. The later re-discovery of the great Reformers brought together a group of young Methodist scholars who had studied in Germany in the early years of the Third Reich. Led by Gordon Rupp, Philip Watson, Percy Scott, Stanley Frost (who later served in Canada) and Rupert Davies, they showed that to talk of the 'Catholicity of Protestantism' was not to talk nonsense but to explore a much wider churchmanship which held together justification by faith and traditional Wesleyan theology with a wider application of classical Protestantism. As we shall see, this came to fruition after the war.

## 4. The Second World War and after

War came in 1939. There was no cheering in the streets as in August 1914. Indeed the cheering had been for Neville Chamberlain after 'Munich' in 1938. We, literally, went on digging the air-raid shelter in our garden. The Methodist Church had its pacifists – honoured men like Donald Soper, Henry Carter and Henry Bett (President 1940) – but most accepted the just war concept, gritting their teeth for a long conflict with Hitler. The war affected Methodism in many ways, not always easy to define. The 'black out' affected patterns of worship. The swing to morning worship began at this time. Many of the younger men were in the armed services which meant that Sunday Schools were often dominated by elderly people. At the time their help was welcome; later it became a cause of great concern. Younger ministers served as chaplains, recruitment to ordained ministry ceased, the theological colleges were closed. Local preaching was in transition, with many more women taking up and enriching the work of preaching. On the debit side, however, many well- meaning men and women who were not adequately trained became accredited preachers.

War damage poleaxed the work of the churches in city areas.[5] 2,600 buildings were destroyed or damaged, 214 chapels and 24 manses were destroyed in the blitz of 1940–1 and many more later, with an estimated £2,000,000 (1940 values) of damage. Work in the inner city areas of London never really revived. In 1938 there were 108 mission centres, and only 8 escaped damage. In 1950 there were 76 London mission churches in the inner belt, and a generation later those working in these areas experienced a feeling of isolation and lack of representation within wider Methodism.

W. E. Sangster carried out a notable war time ministry in the large shelter [13] beneath the Central Hall in Westminster, writing his doctoral thesis on Christian Perfection in the small hours! This ministry

was paralleled by Donald Soper at Kingsway Hall and others in innumerable mission centres in London and the blitzed areas of most cities and towns. Country chapels found hospitality for evacuees from the towns. Local and national ecumenism was enhanced by the blitz with William Temple, who was Archbishop of Canterbury from 1942 to 1944, seeing through the birth of the British Council of Churches in 1942.

---

13. When I began my ministry in Westminster, I did not receive a single word of greeting from any neighbouring church. Not one! It is unimportant, of course, but it seemed rather unfriendly to a man, who though a Londoner, had had the good fortune to spend his early ministry in the provinces. The bombing altered that and gave expression to a kindliness I am sure was already there. The Dean of Westminster sent his good wishes across the road. The genial Bishop of Kensington spent a night in one of our shelters. Bishop Mathew (Cardinal Hinsley's coadjutor) came in for a couple of hours. The Rector of the parish has addressed us in the shelter below, and in the church above. The Roman Catholic priest slips in to see his own people and has won a secure place in our hearts. More than ever we believe in the Holy Catholic and Apostolic Church.

*Source*: W. E. Sangster cited in P. Sangster *Dr Sangster*, Epworth Press 1962, p. 137.

---

There was a genuine sense of unity during the war and after it some resurgence of faith and confidence, especially in the universities, which has not been seen since. The destruction of war led to the reconstruction of more than 2,607 damaged churches for which upwards of half a million pounds came from the War Damage Compensation and £600,000 from Methodism. The work of Benson Perkins and Albert Hearn at the Chapel Department was of vital importance, as was the support given by the Rank Trust. Methodism owed much to the Ranks, father and son, though bingo caused a rift in the lute! 'We must plan or perish,' said Perkins. The story of the re-structuring of Methodist work in London and later of its development in New Towns deserves a book of its own. Could there be a reconstruction of faith?

Styles of evangelism changed. In the 1930s, characteristically, Henry Carter pioneered a youth movement called the Youth and Christian Citizenship Movement in which young people were challenged to look at and make resolutions over a range of social issues, including peace, war, and the social order, as well as drink and gambling. It was a pointer to a new style of Christian ethical involvement. The Korean war was for many who had not been directly involved in World War Two a turning point on the pacifist issue. Henry Carter himself moved in its direction through the 1930s, becoming one of the pioneers, alongside Bishop Bell, of the churches' concern for refugees and the reconstruction of Germany. Like William W. Simpson, who was Secretary of the Council of Christians and Jews, he deserves a place in the history of radical ecumenism.

During and after the war Colin Roberts (1886–1975), who became Home Mission Secretary in 1939, initiated Christian Commando Campaigns with the slogan 'New men for a New age'. They ended in 1947 but enabled many lay people, as well as young ministers like Bill Gowland, to take their faith to their fellows at work, a style only possible perhaps in the constrictions of war. Gowland (1911–1991) became aware of the great gulf between church and working people, a concern which after the war led to his splendid evangelistic ministry at the Albert Hall Manchester, and later to the Luton Industrial Mission. Young men like Richard Jones and Harry Morton, future Presidents of Conference, caught their vision from Gowland. In the 1930s there emerged the figure of Donald Soper (born 1903) who in 1998 still preaches at Hinde Street and still speaks in Hyde Park, an open air ministry begun on Tower Hill in 1927! Soper was appointed to Kingsway Hall in 1936, and there he combined a sacramental theology with a profound conviction of the possibility of democratic socialism and an ardent pacifism. He was the epitome of much of the best in Methodism at the time [14].

> 14. I yearn for a return to the kind of Christianity which is first of all a searching of our hearts that we may discover his new way of life, a Christianity which today would set out to translate the words of Jesus for this twentieth century so that we could see the footprints of the Master along the streets of London and Moscow and Peking and New York . . . and walking in these footmarks could be content with the iron rations of adventure . . . Worship is the soil in which faith and works can grow.
>
> *Source*: Donald Soper, *Aflame with Faith*, Epworth Press 1963, pp. 77–78.

Many of the younger generation were schooled in evangelism by Donald Soper in the Order of Christian Witness (OCW), which held campaigns in towns and rural areas (Newcastle, Exeter etc.) showing the relevance of the corporate and sacramental as well as the individual component in evangelism. That this method seems to be superseded could, I fear, be to the church's loss. Adrian Hastings did not exaggerate when he said of the post-war period: 'The Methodism of these men was as enlightened, mature, outgoing and faithful a form of Christianity as one might find anywhere.'[6] That was the mood after the horrors of a World War.

## For discussion

1. Do the old divisions of Methodism matter any more now? What difference did Methodist union make in your area?
2. Have we withdrawn too easily from inner city and town areas? Can we 'plant' churches there now?
3. Why are people so reluctant ever to close a place of worship?
4. Did Methodism place too much stress on avoiding drinking and gambling? How do we deal *now* with personal moral evil?
5. Describe the life of your church. What are the various groups and functions for? Have we changed much from the descriptions of Grainger's Lane, Beckminster and Cockleford?
6. What should be the role now of various groups within Methodism – Headway, Alliance of Radical Methodism, Methodist Sacramental Fellowship etc.?

# 3
# Methodism 1950–1998

## 1. The 1950s

The period after World War Two was paradoxically a time of renewed hopes and then, later, more sober assessment. There did not seem to be the disillusionment which marked the time after the First World War. The Labour Administration under Clement Attlee made the 'welfare state' (the phrase originated with Alfred Zimmern and was popularized by William Temple) a reality, carrying out many of the recommendations of the Beveridge Report of 1942 on social security which aimed at ridding society of the five 'giants' of 'want, sickness, squalor, ignorance and idleness'. A report to Conference, *The Message and Mission of Methodism* (1946), followed later by the *Missionary Obligation of the Church* (1955), set the tone, re-affirming the Wesleyan emphasis in theology, stated in a reasonably modern style, and stressing the need for much deeper fellowship and spirituality and for the renewal of worship. At the time youth work was still strong, and there were opportunities in worship which could satisfy both the sacramental and the more evangelistic in the ministry, with a confident biblical theology. There seemed considerable consensus and little party strife. Calls for evangelism culminated in a Year of Evangelism in 1952. Despite W. E. Sangster's herculean efforts this did not have the flair of the Christian Commando Campaigns and was overshadowed later by Billy Graham. Soon Donald Soper was asking if Methodism was a dying church. After a slight increase in the post-war decade membership had begun to fall. Sangster asserted in *Methodism, Her Unfinished Task* (1947) the need to spread scriptural holiness, to evangelize, to redeem rural areas, to teach the use of money, and to enlist the service of lay people. This suited the mood of the time. A much publicized sermon illustrated the basic pietism of the approach. What would revival bring to Britain? It would primarily exalt the Lord but the consequences would be many [15].

> 15. 1. It would Pay Old Debts.
> 2. It would Reduce Sexual Immorality.
> 3. It would Disinfect the Theatre.
> 4. It would Cut the Divorce Rate.
> 5. It would Reduce Juvenile Crime.
> 6. It would Lessen the Prison Population.
> 7. It would Improve the Quality and Increase the Output of Work.
> 8. It would Restore to the Nation a Sense of High Destiny.
> 9. It would Make us Invincible in the War of Ideas.
> 10. It would give Happiness and Peace to the People.
>
> *Source*: A sermon preached by Dr Sangster on 4 January 1953, quoted by P. Sangster, *Dr Sangster*, Epworth Press 1962, p. 173.

The more Catholic-minded Methodists, noting among young ministers and some lay people a greater attention to worship and especially holy communion, more use of the corpus of the Wesley hymns than had been the case for a decade or two, and a growing stress on group fellowship, felt that their time had come. Biblical theology seemed to provide a critical orthodoxy which was preachable – see, for example, the report on *Doctrinal Preaching* (1951) written by Gordon Rupp. Systematic theologians from other traditions like John and Donald Baillie and Herbert Farmer backed up the biblical studies of C. H. Dodd, T. W. Manson and Vincent Taylor. Not a few entered the ordained ministry with high hopes. Methodism seemed to unite the best of Protestantism and Catholicism, its worship combining the insights of the liturgical movement and of more evangelistic approaches. Cliff College and Donald Soper, after all, were happily together in Methodism.

There were areas, moreover, where Methodism was growing – indeed in this period two churches were opened each week. Examples from one area will show the need to analyse a longish period, not just that of post-war growth. In the early 1950s Trinity Circuit in Wolverhampton 'planted' a church on the Springdale Estate. Initially members were transferred from the strong Beckminster church, but some imported leaders withdrew when local leaders had been trained and equipped. That was in 1952. At about the same time a young Irish couple went to live on the Rake Gate Estate. From their initiative and circuit help, a new church was built there. It flourished, attracting a large number of young people, but it went into the doldrums as the population aged. Sociological factors condition the life of any church! In the 1980s work among elderly people flourished. Now, again, the population is more youthful. A small 'free church' at Codsall, a developing suburb, came into the circuit and grew into a strong church. The story needs balancing with the closure twenty years on of Trinity, the circuit church, which H. H. Fowler, Lord Wolverhampton, the first Methodist cabinet minister, had attended. But an innerbelt church, Cranmer, has transformed itself into a resource for reaching the needs of the poor and handicapped. This takes us well beyond the 1950s into the very different ethos of the 1980s. The Wolverhampton story, however, reflects the fact that the West Midlands conurbation can be taken as a most striking example of post-war suburban growth and later industrial decline. Sociological factors underlie and condition both growth and decline.

But – to return to the 1950s – all was not well. The report on *Rural Methodism* (1958) made the blunt assertion that 'one out of every seven services are conducted by unofficial and irregular speakers many of whom do not believe or teach our doctrines but whose services are tolerated by both people and ministers because otherwise the pulpit would remain empty'. This was one of the many problems, especially in winning young people for discipleship, in areas where between one third and one half of Methodist members still lived. Ministers were criticized for lack of a proper pastoral policy. 'Methodism is already paying a heavy price for poverty of worship and preaching. Unless there is drastic improvement it will destroy Methodism as we know it.' This was a gloomy but realistic picture. The beginning of a proper system of travel allowance for ministers followed at a time when, as a young minister in a rural circuit, I 'clocked up' 3,000 miles per annum on a bicycle! John Lawson's *Green and Pleasant Land* was more positive, as was the Shropshire Border Experiment and the later work of Jack Lucas. In more recent times both the Church of England, with the *Faith in the Countryside* report, and the Arthur Rank Centre, through the work of Anthony Russell and John Clarke, have shown that pessimism need not dominate the scene. But there has been great frustration in many rural circuits, not least due to depopulation and vast changes in agriculture. Ecumenism was often rudimentary in many rural areas in the 1950s. Subsequently canon B15A allowed members of other communions to share in Anglican eucharists, though confirmation was still required for full participation in the parish church, and was a most important factor.

Membership figures since 1951 [16] make salutary reading. They need, of course, to be correlated with population changes, birthrates and sizes of congregation (as distinct from membership) to give a full picture, but provide a silent commentary on fifty years of vast changes in culture and lifestyle which affected many organizations beside the churches.

| 16. | *Membership Figures* | | |
|---|---|---|---|
| 1950 | 744,815 | 1975 | 557,329 |
| 1955 | 744,321 | 1980 | 487,572 |
| 1960 | 728,589 | 1985 | 456,527 |
| 1965 | 690,347 | 1990 | 424,540 |
| 1970 | 617,018 | 1995 | 380,195 |

*Source*: *The Minutes of Conference* for the year following in each case.

## 2. The 1960s and the consequences

The 1960s are most difficult to summarize. Adrian Hastings bluntly states 'The mid 1950s can be dated pretty precisely as the end of the age of preaching; people suddenly ceased to think it worthwhile listening to a special preacher' and then 'Methodism in the 1960s, while awaiting union, had little history except for an unprecedented rate of numerical decline. At the end it was left with only a smack in the face.'[1] There is some truth here but it felt rather more exciting to be a minister in Sheffield and Leeds than that! The story varies according to the vantage point from which it is told.

'From the top' there could appear confusion, and the possibilities of new ecclesiastical alignments loomed large. The number of candidates for the ordained ministry – not only in Methodism, of course – declined dramatically, with grave organizational effects. Wesley College at Headingley in Leeds closed in 1966, the buildings being sold to the Little Sisters of the Poor and the college itself being united with Didsbury College in Bristol, which was renamed 'Wesley College'. Richmond College in London, famous for its missionary associations – the German theologian and opponent of Hitler, Dietrich Bonhoeffer, had bowed in solemn remembrance at the Memorial in the Hall – closed in 1971. Later, after considerable and acrimonious controversy, Hartley Victoria College in Manchester also closed, though the staff and students, having found a temporary home at Northern Baptist College, were able in 1982 to join a federal structure for ministerial training in Manchester. A very positive and speedy move was the amalgamation of the Methodist Handsworth College, Birmingham with the Anglican Queen's College under the Principalship of John Habgood, who was later to be Bishop of Durham and then Archbishop of York. This venture provided England with its only fully ecumenical theological college. With hindsight some of the closures seem premature and even panicky – and it is no consolation to realize that they were not unique to Methodism.

Since 1970 the situation has changed dramatically. First, the ordination of women was at last accepted. There had been bitter controversy in 1948 – Russell Maltby was even shouted down in Conference – and while the Anglican–Methodist conversations took place an expedient moratorium, supported by Miss Pauline Webb and others involved in both causes, had been observed. But in 1972 the vote was decisive. Secondly, the Wesley Deaconess Order for a time ceased to recruit new members, but was later opened to men as well as women, becoming the Methodist Diaconal Order with 120 ordained and probationer members in 1995. The 1970s, in fact, saw a new style of ministry emerging. Thirdly, in the early 1970s ecumenical hopes were dashed. Methodist leaders had seemed sure that the Anglican–Methodist conversations would produce new possibilities of ministry and mission, and their confidence was shared by the more radical elements in the church. Such hopes were flattened in 1969 and 1972 when the Church of England's Convocations and Synod could not secure a sufficient majority for the scheme for union.

From the 'bottom' the situation looked different. Theologically there was the challenge of books like John Robinson's *Honest to God* (1963), which, confused though it was, became a symbol of new thinking and had a positive side. It became possible to face doubt head on, not pretending to hold beliefs no longer feasible. It was possible, too, in very ordinary churches to share in new styles of worship. New liturgies were at last being produced, the Renewal Group liturgy being one among many. New ballads, such as those of Sydney Carter, could be sung in church. It is interesting that only one of these, 'One more step along the world I go', survived into *Hymns and Psalms* (1983). These songs, like 'When I needed a neighbour' and 'Lord of the Dance', represented a new mood of contemporaneity and secular concern – indeed 'secular' was the great inword then. Richard Jones, then in Sheffield, gave us

> God of concrete, God of steel,
> God of motorway and wheel . . .
> All the world of power is thine.

To be in Sheffield at that time was exhilarating as well as mind-blowing. The community desperately needed integration as vast housing complexes, built with a political idealism which had tragically little contact with the needs of ordinary people, hit the skyline. In such a situation, new theologies linked with new styles of outreach and new possibilities of ecumenism opened up. We even had our own Faith and Order Committee in the city to assist the powerful Council of Churches.

For some the old system was intolerable, for others redeemable. The Renewal Group (1961) enabled a number of younger ministers and lay folk to support one another in difficult, puzzling, but exciting times. Some typical convictions are expressed [17] by Dr John Vincent, at that time Superintendent of the Champress Hall, Rochdale. A glance through the forgotten pages of the radical magazine *New Directions* (1964–69) is both fascinating and disturbing. Some of the best ideas seem to have run into the ground. Others have been much more fruitful.

One fruitful concept was the notion of 'team ministry' of which the outstanding example was the Notting Hill Team Ministry led by Geoffrey Ainger, David Mason and Norwyn Denny on the initiative of Donald Soper. It was a positive aftermath to the Notting Hill race riots of 1958, and opened up a rich social ministry in a multi-racial area. Much more experiment in worship and pastoral care was possible than in a 'normal' church, though now it seems heavily ministerial. Another example is found in Leeds. The Oxford Place Mission and Brunswick Church – two great historic churches – amalgamated in 1968. They were able to support a superintendent minister, an associate minister who was full-time chaplain in the university and polytechnic, a proba-

tioner minister who was able to promote youth work in the crypt, and a deaconess who headed up pastoral work not only to a large church membership but to the needs of inner city Leeds in collaboration with St George's church, which did fine work among the disadvantaged. In all these projects there were problems and tensions – of authority, group dynamics and personality. Much has been learned, not least about the inadequacy of purely clerical teams. The Leeds Mission now has a lay organizer.

From the sociological thinking of the 1960s came plans for a new Methodist constitution with Divisions [18] rather than Departments 'at the top' and at

---

**17.**

1. Christ is where his deeds are done; and the disciple is called to *service*.
2. Christ is where his ministry of healing and redemption is continued; and the disciple is called to *healing*.
3. Christ is being dealt with, ministered unto or rejected in the person of others – hidden within the secular – and the disciple is called to *recognition*.
4. Christ is on the cross; and the disciple is called to *suffering*.
5. Christ is ruling his universe, both openly and secretly; and the disciple is called to *indication*.

*Source*: John J. Vincent, *Secular Christ*, Lutterworth Press 1968, p. 218.

---

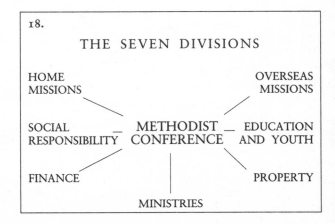

**18.**

### THE SEVEN DIVISIONS

HOME MISSIONS

OVERSEAS MISSIONS

SOCIAL RESPONSIBILITY — METHODIST CONFERENCE — EDUCATION AND YOUTH

FINANCE

PROPERTY

MINISTRIES

local level an end to the twin rule of 'trustees' and 'leaders'. The Church Council was to replace trustees' and leaders' meetings, not only acting as 'managing trustees' of the local church property, but also giving spiritual leadership. Subordinate committees dealt with pastoral matters, property, mission, neighbourhood, church family, etc. In 1976, despite dogged opposition in some quarters, The Methodist Church Act gave some of these changes statutory undergirding in what appeared to be a more effective managerial style of running the church. Experience was to prove, however, that the local church would still have too many committees. By the 1990s the slogan was 'committees meet, teams act'. Out were to go permanent committees, in would come *ad hoc* working parties. Experience also proved that some of the fellowship associated with the old Quarterly Meeting, which, especially in rural circuits had often been preceded by an informal meal, drained away. Many of the ideas of the 1960s, in fact, being based on the secular fashion of the 1950s, now appear intolerably bureaucratic.

To some outside it, no church seems to have more rules and regulations or more obsessive forward planning than Methodism. The vicar, who wants the Methodist minister to preach next Sunday at Evensong and doesn't realize that the circuit 'plan', that unique Methodist document, was made months ago, doubtless finds the system a 'bugbear'. The 'plan', incidentally, shows that Methodism is a 'connexion', not a collection of independent churches. In the 1990s, however, the principle of 'subsidiarity' reigns. Small is beautiful, the local is determinative. Having been obliged to work with overloaded 'set' agendas, we are now told [19] that the constitution is too complex. Local churches and circuits may now organize themselves in some spheres as they wish. One area, however, the training of Local Preachers, is still uniform because they must be able to operate anywhere in the Methodist Church.

Mission must determine church structures. Inspired pragmatism was, after all, Wesley's characteristic stance. So replacing the seven 'Divisions' will be

---

19. The present arrangements . . . go back to the 1970s and in recent years have proved less than adequate to a changed situation. Perceptions and relationships have changed and the sense has grown that what is needed is a more flexible and open system . . . The evident need is for greater simplicity: an orderly framework which will provide room for future adaptation. There is no single correct way to structure any organisation. When frustrations build up in an organisation, however, there is a strong danger that structures which are means to ends will become ends in themselves. So the desire is for a coherent structure which will set the church free to address its present needs and functions.

*Source*: *The Methodist Conference Agenda*, 1992, Vol. 2, pp. 608–10.

---

connexional team leaders heading up four major areas of concern [20].

Links with circuits and local churches will be vital if any new connexional system is to work smoothly.

---

20.

*Methodist Conference*

Methodist Council Executive

The Methodist Council

1  Church Life                    3  Church and Society

2  Inter-Church and            4  Administrative
   Other Relationships            Services

---

The role of the new Methodist Council, which replaces the older General Purposes Committee and the more recent President's Council, will be vital as an overall barometer of opinion and as an advisory body. It has been given considerable power alongside Conference.

## 3. Changes in spirituality

It is fascinating to the historian that 1963, the year of *Honest to God*, was also the year in which the Charismatic Movement began to be noticeable in the mainstream churches. As in the eighteenth century, revival and reason can emerge together. Methodism was significantly influenced by the new movement in the 1970s when there was a resurgence of the 'religion of the heart', so despised by the radicals, and of an evangelicalism, conservative in style and with a tendency to Pentecostalism, which contrasted with the renewed Wesleyanism of the 1940s and 1950s. 'Worship songs' began to eclipse both Wesley and Sydney Carter alike! There is no doubt that many found a liberation of spirit, thanks to a stress on immediacy and an expression of feeling not found in the rather didactic styles which had become normative.

There is no doubt, too, that the last generation, of whatever theological persuasion, had neglected the doctrine of the Holy Spirit, and that therefore through a renewal of the gifts of the Spirit some have been helped to a richer spirituality, which has been accompanied by a renewal of interest in the sacraments. Indeed, it is possible in Methodism to combine the maximum of traditional styles – corporate prayer, meaningful symbolism, colour and light – with maximum spontaneity, whether in an act of worship or at a fellowship or conference meeting, not just to please or appease all but because of the sheer attractiveness of the mix. The historian David Bebbington shows how all this runs parallel with cultural changes in a wider society. The Beatles and Bill Haley and the Comets were more important than *Honest to God* and all that. Counter-cultures, secular and religious, have a strange similarity. There could be more than indirect links between the Charismatic Movement, forms of group awareness, a desire for greater bodily movement in worship and educational styles of self-expression and self-awareness as well as medical insight into the healing of the whole person. Healing – often of psychosomatic conditions – is a feature of charismatic groups. Other cultural changes in sport and popular music are factors too, for the church is never uninfluenced by its environment. The dangers of these developments have been divisiveness and triumphalism on the part of those who claim 'the baptism of the spirit', coupled with intolerance from those who fear too great a stress on specific experiences.

Charismatic groups are often very similar to the groups which were common in young adult and student circles in the 1940s and 1950s before a rather frantic philanthropy took over. Is there now a danger of a kind of pietistic individualism when the stress should be on individuals with 'the gifts' helping the body to enable people to realize the presence of Christ?

Is there a danger of looking too easily for results or for the unusual or bizarre, and of distrusting the normal and the orderliness and stability of a liturgy? Can this lead to the appalling danger of the irrational which represents a breakdown of civilization? The occult, demonology, witchcraft and all manner of theosophy has come in the wake of secularization and post-modernism. Is religion part of a market culture?

On the other hand, if charismatic renewal produces mature, integrated people, then it is of God. Whatever be the positives and negatives of this debate, the charismatic style is a growing feature of world-wide Christianity, and some of Methodism's largest churches are now led by evangelical-charismatics. Perhaps, however, the very pluralism of our Methodist tradition will prevent the total submersion of other styles of faith and worship.

## 4. Changes in ministries and mission

If the 1960s were the time of radicalism, the 1970s saw a renewal of evangelicalism and a new appraisal of the Methodist Church scene. Renewal in the 1960s meant institutional change to foster a 'servant church', the world shaping the agenda with the priority: Christ – the World – the Church. The shift of interest then moved from radicalism to 'liberation' and on to evangelism. The new constitution was put into practice fairly smoothly, with women presbyters taking their place in the ordained ministry. Some found what they felt to be gross prejudice, others, especially perhaps former deaconesses, were able to acclimatize themselves more quickly. On the whole, despite a report brought to Conference in 1995 expressing concern over continuing patriarchy, the contribution of ordained women has been appreciated and has enhanced the breadth of the presbyterate.

A series of important statements expounded the Methodist view of ordained ministry and its relationship to the laity. Statements on Ordination in 1960 and 1974 complement one another, setting out [21] a representative view of ordination which fills out the somewhat negative and defensive position of the Deed of Union.

---

21. . . . it may fairly be said that Methodist Ministers are both travelling preachers in the Methodist Connexion and Ministers of the Word and Sacraments in the Church of God . . . In the office of a minister is brought together the manifold functions of the church's ministry . . . A Methodist minister is a priest, in company with all Christ's faithful people but not all priests are Ministers . . . Ordination is never repeated in the Methodist Church. A Minister is Christ's ambassador and the representative of the whole people of God.

*Source*: 'Ordination in the Methodist Church', *Minutes of Conference*, 1960, pp. 235–42.

---

The 1974 statement took up the 1960 statement and that of a Commission on the Nature of the Church's Ministries, together with the easily forgotten Ordinal of 1968 proposed for the Anglican–Methodist scheme. This statement endorses the view, wrestled with for some time, that it is legitimate for some ministers to find their main sphere of work not in circuit ministry but in a 'sector' of secular life – chaplaincies, education, local government, commerce, medicine etc. There have always been ministers in scholarly appointments, both at home and overseas, but here was a much wider concept. It was clear that some 'sector ministers' had not been happy with what they felt to be the restrictions of a circuit ministry, while others clearly had positive qualifications to serve in a wider sphere so long as they were not doing work better done by lay people – a cause of some confusion. One minister has served as a bus driver with great distinction, but what does that really say about lay bus drivers? In the end a smallish number of ministers have been 'permitted to serve' in 'other appointments', some directed to them, others specifically trained for them. The priesthood of the laity as ambassadors of Christ is spelled out clearly in the reports on *The Ministry of the Whole People of God* (1988) and *On the Ministry of the People of God in the World* (1990). These reports came to a final form in the 1980s but were the result of thinking begun in the 1960s, exploring a much more open and positive view of ministry, which has been increasingly attractive to middle-aged men and women who set off on what Catholic writers have called the 'Second Journey'. Having experienced other professions, they can offer a decade or two of mature life to presbyteral ministry, either in full-time work in a circuit or giving time to the life of the circuit while continuing in a secular occupation. Others, taking early retirement, can give much more time to 'local appointments'. This points to a differentiated presbyterate in the future, contrasting sharply with the nineteenth-century pattern which was influenced by the wider rise of professionalism. Training for ministry today is more practically orientated than in the past, though it is still recognized that a minister must be a 'folk theologian', able to help doubters and faithful alike.

There are significant differences between Methodist ministers and their Anglican or Free Church counterparts. Methodists are ordained in association with Conference, not locally, and normally have a plurality of pastoral units from which to minister, being appointed by Conference to the circuit, not to a local church – a concept now unconsciously being copied by others. Moreover, the relationship between ministers and laity in Methodism is carefully defined. All within the church have the same standing before God and all share in the offering of praise and prayer, self-offering and sacrificial living. Thus, while ministers are recognized as having a representative role and a special authority, the ministry of the laity is strongly affirmed [22].

22. Conference affirms lay ministry in the world as an essential part of the ministry of the church and recognises that in the past it has undervalued lay ministry in the world. It rejoices in the commitment of Christian people in the world recognising that some situations are brutalising and others fulfilling.

*Source*: *On the Ministry of the People of God in the World*, Conference Report 1990.

The emergence of a growing number of full-time lay workers, often doing specialized work, constitutes a further development in the 'ministry'. The overall picture, in fact, is much more complex than anything contemplated by the Deed of Union. Most lay people, needless to say, are in secular occupations, and work out there the sense of vocation to serve the Lord which has always been at the heart of Protestant and Methodist theology. In an age of frequent job changes and unemployment, however, how calling and responsibility are understood will need rigorous rethinking.

During this period the role of the laity came into proper prominence. In the 1960s the Laymen's Movement and later the Board of Lay Training, led for a time by Dr Pauline Webb, sought to show that the church was a partnership in which the ordained should help 'the laity' in articulating the Christian witness in the world of work. The Luton Industrial College founded by William Gowland fits into the picture here [23].[2]

23. *Charter of Luton Industrial College*

1. To make the Christian faith relevant in the realms of technology and industry and commerce.
2. To give training in industrial mission, not only in theory but in practice.
3. Whilst it is a Christian enterprise, it is not for Christians only but anyone willing to consider the claims of Christ as Lord and the needs of the world.

Maybe some of these emphases appear rather masculine, but there needs to be increasing concern at the lack of appeal to *men* of much contemporary church life.

This in no way denigrates the much more planned work among women. The organization of Women's Work (of the Methodist Missionary Society) began in 1858 as 'the Ladies Committee for the Amelioration of the Condition of Women in Heathen Countries, Female Education etc . . .' Later, under the formidable Caroline Wiseman, it spearheaded the training and equipping of missionaries, doctors and nurses, and facilitated the educational enterprise which enabled a whole church to engage in mission. This style continued well after the Second World War, backed up with work among younger women in the Girls' League which, after its demise in 1955, sought a wider constituency in the Youth Missionary Association.

During the war a rather different style, under the auspices of Home Mission, saw the blossoming of the Women's Fellowship, which sponsored young wives' groups and residential work among single mothers and their children. The aim was defined as 'to foster a Christian womanhood which sees life whole and undivided.' Ideas came from the USA in this area. If young wives' groups flourished, however, some single women rightly felt that their role was undervalued. A younger generation, too, did not fit easily into older patterns which assumed a nuclear two-parent family as the norm. The consequence of much heart searching was the creation of the Women's Network of the Methodist Church (1987) with its new magazine *Magnet* which, along with *Connect*, replaced the older missionary magazines, *The Kingdom Overseas* and later *Now*. These developments reflect the new partnership styles which have replaced outmoded mission ideas associated with the days of the British Empire. The idea of facilitating 'networks' of involved lay people in various spheres – medicine, commerce, industry, education – has long been the concern of David Clark of Westhill College, and it could still come into its own in the more flexible organization of Methodism, reflecting secular change in management, which began to operate in 1996. The Conference office and a Methodist Council, elected by Conference and with its own executive, will link with four connexional Team Leaders with responsibilities in the areas of Church Life, Church and Society, Inter-church Relationships and Central Services, including property and money. The acid test of all the changes – which to some look like St Vitus' Dance – will be whether the connexional style, which differentiated Methodism from the 'gathered church' of the Free Churches, can be maintained. If this disintegrates, Methodism, as usually understood, will have disappeared.

## 5. Citizenship and sexuality

Since the Second World War, the work of the Social Responsibility Department and Division has been notable – Carter and Urwin were followed by secretaries of the calibre of Edward Rogers and Kenneth Greet, and much valuable work was done behind the scenes rather than through resolutions brought to Conference. A stream of constructive reports did not perhaps gain the publicity they deserved. We will look at the area of changes in sexual practice and the breakdown of the nuclear family. In 1962 Professor G. M. Carstairs said that 'charity was now more important than chastity'. Methodism's stance in this period was one of commonsense and openness to new insights. Three examples can be given.

The first is the report on *Abortion* (1976) which avoids the hardline Catholic view, which stresses the total humanity of the foetus, and the liberal line, which gives the potential mother absolute rights. The Abortion Act of 1967 is welcomed but a number of valuable points are made [24]. Some doctors have found this report to be a good working statement of criteria.

The second example is a full revision of the statement on *The Christian View of Marriage and the Family* of 1939 which was published in 1992 as a *Christian Understanding of Family Life, the Single Person and Marriage*. The report is worth careful study as it combines commonsense, liberality and a consistent advocacy of the 'well tested basic principles of chastity before marriage and faithfulness after-

> **24.** Abortions should be limited to the first twenty weeks of pregnancy save in exceptional cases (such as the dire risk to the life of the mother or severe abnormality). Counselling must be offered in all cases. The profit motive must be reduced . . . abortion must not be regarded as an alternative to contraception nor is it to be justified merely as a method of birth control. The termination of any form of human life can never be regarded superficially and should not be available on demand but should remain subject to a legal framework, to responsible counselling and to medical judgement. In an imperfect world when both individuals and society will often fail, abortion may be seen as a necessary way of mitigating the results of these failures. It does not remove the urgent need to seek remedies for the causes of these failures.
>
> *Source*: *Declarations and Statements*, Methodist Church Division of Social Responsibility 1983, pp. 1–4.

wards. These offer the most fitting ways of discovering the rich meaning of sexual union in the one flesh'. The increasing tendency of couples to cohabit is not dodged. 'Many Christian couples now live together before marriage . . . and other Christians unable to marry for varied reasons are deeply committed to each other and find expression of their love in sexual intercourse . . . in these situations understanding and a sense of proportion and awareness of the modern sexual climate are needed as well as the affirmation of Christian values.'

This statement was overshadowed by the discussion which preceded and followed the *Statement on Human Sexuality* (1990) and an earlier statement of 1980, used as a study document without full Conference affirmation. The 1993 major resolutions need to be set out [25] for the sake of clarity and proper discussion.

In a church with diverse theological opinions this statement could hardly hope to claim unanimous support. It was the result of deep debate between some concerned to uphold what they saw as clear scriptural norms and others convinced that human knowledge, undreamed of in the days of St Paul, is also relevant. It needs to be realized that other churches, and notably the Church of England, have gone through or are

25.

1.      The Conference, affirming the joy of human sexuality as God's gift and the place of every human being within the grace of God, recognizes the responsibility that flows from this for us all. It therefore welcomes the serious, prayerful and sometimes costly consideration given to this issue by the Methodist Church.

2.      All practices of sexuality which are promiscuous, exploitative or demeaning in any way are unacceptable forms of behaviour and contradict God's purposes for us all.

3.      A person shall not be debarred from the church on the grounds of sexual orientation in itself.

4.      The Conference reaffirms the traditional teaching of the Church on human sexuality; namely chastity for all outside marriage and fidelity within it. The Conference directs that this affirmation is made clear to all candidates for ministry, office and membership, and having established this affirms that the existing procedures of our church are adequate to deal with all such cases.

5.      The Conference resolves that its decisions in this debate shall not be used to form the basis of a disciplinary charge against any person in relation to conduct alleged to have taken place before such decisions were made.

6.      Conference recognizes, affirms and celebrates the participation and ministry of lesbians and gay men in the church. Conference calls on the Methodist people to begin a pilgrimage of faith to combat repression and discrimination, to work for justice and human rights and to give dignity and worth to people whatever their sexuality.

*Source*: Methodist Conference, *Minutes*, 1993, pp. 1–2.

involved in the same process. In all churches there is a tendency now for advocates of the 'Evangelical' position to have greater confidence. Ministers trained in the 1960s tended to be rather more liberal than those who are now, quite properly, moving into positions of high responsibility.

In Methodism, however, the centrality of the person of Jesus Christ provides a focus for unity which transcends 'liberal' and 'conservative' theological viewpoints.

## For discussion

1. Do you think the church lost its confidence after 1960? Why?
2. If you are in a rural church, what are your hopes and fears? What of ecumenical possibilities?
3. What contributions do ministers in 'the sectors' and ministers in 'local appointment' make? Do we really need paid ordained ministers now?
4. Do you think the constitution of 1974 has worked? If not, why not? Do you think the new set up, brought into operation in 1996, will be any more effective?
5. Estimate and evaluate the Charismatic Movement's influence on Methodism, drawing where possible on personal testimony.
6. Was the statement on abortion of 1976 too liberal? Why?
7. How does a church with varied views on human sexuality hold together?
8. Is the centrality of Christ a matter which brings together 'evangelicals', 'radicals' and 'liberals'? How? Why?

# 4

# Methodism and the Wider World

## 1. Social responsibility

We now ask how Methodism has related to the events and ideologies of the modern world: Nazism, World War Two, Cold War and Apartheid, for example, not to mention the fall of Communism in Russia, so unexpected and bewildering to the intelligentsia. As we do so, two things should be noted at the outset: first, as James Munson has pointed out [26], the relationship between the institutional decline of English Nonconformity, on the one hand, and its continuing influence, on the other, is not easy to fathom;[1] and, second, by 1996 the number of Free Church members was beginning to rise, especially in the Pentecostal and Evangelical churches.

26. The decline of English Nonconformity as a major part of English culture in the twentieth century may well be seen as being as profound a change in English history as the suppression of the monasteries under Henry VIII ... However, unlike the monasteries, Nonconformity's influence has survived its institutional decline. Indeed, it has so permeated English life in the twentieth century that the Nonconformist legacy has affected millions who have never set foot inside a chapel.

*Source*: J. Munson, *The Nonconformists In Search of a Lost Culture*, SPCK 1991, p. 1.

In 1932, as we have seen, Methodism seemed at a superficial glance to be desperately concerned about personal moral issues and Conference resolutions appeared to be almost knee-jerk reactions of no weight outside a smallish circle. But the wider concerns of theologians like W. F. Lofthouse and the veteran S. E. Keeble (1853–1946) were beginning to claim the attention of Henry Carter and Clifford Urwin. A statement on *The Christian View of Industry in Relation to Social Order*, which appeared in 1934, clearly reflected the influence of the notable Birmingham Conference of 1924 on *Christian Politics, Economics and Citizenship* (COPEC), chaired by William Temple, in which Methodists like S. E. Keeble, W. F. Lofthouse, C. Ryder Smith and Benson Perkins played a leading role. Statements on employment (though nothing as massive as *Men Without Work*, 450 pages in 1938 by the Pilgrim Trust) were backed up by support for the unemployed in County Durham and elsewhere in their fearful poverty. The general mood favoured a mildly corporate style of welfare state.

An important statement on *Marriage and the Family* in 1939 was extended by a statement on *Divorce and the Law of Marriage* after the war. The family statement (totally revised and replaced in 1992) was very positive about the role of sexuality

> 27. In the light of New Testament principles and teaching . . . the Methodist Church is at one with other Christian communions in affirming as the norm and standard of Christian marriage the lifelong and exclusive union of one man and one woman.
>
> *Source*: *Declarations of Conference on Social Questions*, Epworth Press 1959, p. 87.

in the context of a 'lifelong and exclusive union' [27].

No Christian church at the time would have done other than affirm chastity outside marriage and fidelity within it, though the paragraph on the unmarried now seems very outmoded. Contraception is accepted with reservations. In the report *The Re-Marriage of Divorced Persons* (1948) there is a reminder that an 'innocent' party may remarry (Standing Order 109, *Minutes of Conference*, 1937). This referred to overseas churches but clearly was of universal application. The custom therefore arose of permitting such remarriages, if the minister or – and here is the conscience clause – a colleague was happy to conduct the ceremony. There is a paradox here. 'Protestant' churches, such as Methodism, tend to be strict on some moral issues, like the use of alcohol, gambling and Sunday observance, while appearing more liberal on matters like marriage, divorce and the family. Certainly the help of the Methodist church and its ministers over the matter of marriage, which many people have sought, is part of a considerable pastoral ministry to those with whom otherwise there would have been no contact. The more 'Catholic' churches have always appeared to be stricter on these matters. The Church of England did not give clear approval of contraception till as late as 1948, and Roman Catholics allow annulment of marriage but never divorce or remarriage while a partner is alive. We have already seen how these matters developed after the sexual revolution of the 1960s, the Methodist Kenneth Greet playing a key role in the significant BCC report *Sex and Morality* (1966). Edward Norman's question continues to challenge: Do the churches respond to social changes driven by secular forces or have they something unique to declare?

## 2. War, peace and politics

What was the political allegiance of Methodists before the war? The old alliance of Nonconformity and Liberalism was dead, though many Methodists still voted Liberal. Increasingly, younger ministers were Labour voters, and not a few of the middle class people supported conservatism or at least the National Government. Lloyd George made an attempt to arouse Nonconformist support for what was, in effect, his last bid for power in 1935. The *Call to Action* and its council, said Stephen Koss,[2] was surely one of the most hopelessly misconceived modern political enterprises. Scott Lidgett was involved in this. He could fairly be accused of political blundering but it is an almost forgotten incident. In the election of 1935 Methodist Liberals like Isaac Foot left the corridors of power for ever, and Lloyd George even expressed a transitory admiration for Hitler! In the North East, particularly, the rapport of Methodism with the Labour Party was much stronger [28].

> 28. I grew up in a West Durham village that still exerts considerable influence on my life. The chapel was my social centre as well as a training ground and a place of worship . . . the Methodist Church was the forum for discussion and action which involved every aspect of life in the local community. Here men who were denied recognition at work found dignity, self respect and confidence . . . This was the working man's church, an effective force in society carrying the gospel into daily life . . . Methodists were not given permission to take part in politics, they were expected to do so.
>
> *Source*: Ernest Armstrong MP, *Vice-Presidential Address to the Methodist Conference*, 1974.

Arthur Henderson, the first Labour Foreign Secretary, who died in 1935, was an active Methodist member. Philip Snowdon, Chancellor of the Exchequer, also had Methodist allegiance. He spoke of the great influence of S. E. Keeble. Later cabinet ministers in the Attlee administration – Jack Lawson (Lord Lawson), Ellen Wilkinson and George Tomlinson, the last two successive Ministers of Education – were Methodist members. They have their successors in well-known figures like Len Murray (Lord Murray), George Thomas (Lord Tonypandy), Paul Boateng and Hilary Armstrong, with Selwyn Lloyd and more recently Sir Rhodes Boyson on the other side. It is interesting that three successive post-war Speakers of the House of Commons – Selwyn Lloyd, Dr Horace King and George Thomas – were Methodists, with Ernest Armstrong a Deputy Speaker. Were Methodists the mediators rather than political hardliners? Alan Beith maintains the style of Methodist presence among the Liberal Democrats.

Politicians among the Vice-Presidents of the Methodist Conference have not been numerous, but they include Sir Robert Perks (1932), Isaac Foot (1937), George Thomas (1960) and Ernest Armstrong (1974). At local government level the number of Methodists who are councillors is not as high as it was at the turn of the century but people like James Whittaker, Mayor of Wolverhampton in 1935, and Alan S. Brigg, Mayor of Bolton in 1983, both practising Methodists, made – and continue to make – invaluable contributions. A new town in the North West, Peterlee, is named after Peter Lee (1864–1935), a typical Primitive Methodist politician – Local Preacher, County Councillor and Alderman, Magistrate and MP. The Justice of the Peace who is a Methodist is far from uncommon – there have recently been four in my local church in Lancashire. There is now no unified Methodist political stance, though some Methodist activists occasionally speak and act as though there were. As a result, an ominous gap often yawns between Conference activists, ready to move Notices of Motion on everything under the sun, and the rank and file of the church, taking little notice of most of such proposals but nevertheless very concerned about moral and political issues.

We have already seen that the 1930s are surprisingly difficult to summarize. It was a period of depression and unemployment, and of the consequent attraction of Fascism and Marxism. In Roman Catholicism, because a growing number of younger people entered higher education, the emergence of a new Catholic intelligentsia was paralleled, in some quarters, by an ominous support for Fascism. There is not a trace of such a development in Methodism. A growing number of Methodists, however, did go to university, and Methodist scholars like Wilbert F. Howard, R. Newton Flew, Vincent Taylor, Herbert Butterfield and Gordon Rupp began exerting an influence, on ministers and laity alike, which extended far beyond denominational and theological boundaries. Pacifism and re-armament divided Methodism as they did other Communions. Conference statements are sparse, though the growth of the RAF was deplored in 1934. Mr Chamberlain was applauded for his work for peace in 1938. We need to remember that such praise was almost universal – Winston Churchill had few Methodist supporters. Pacifists like Donald Soper preferred umbrellas to battleships. The Peace Ballot of 1935 and the Peace Pledge Union of 1935 had much Methodist support. Lady Thatcher was at that time a teenager in Grantham [29].

> **29.** The general political tendency among Methodists and other Nonconformists in our town was generally somewhat to the left wing and even pacifist. Methodists in Grantham were prominent in organizing the 'Peace Ballot' of 1935, circulating a loaded questionnaire to the electorate, which was then declared overwhelmingly to have 'voted for peace'. It was not recorded how far Hitler and Mussolini were moved by the result. We had our views on that in the Roberts family. Being staunchly conservative, we were the odd family. Our friend the Rev Skinner was an enthusiast for the peace ballot. He was the kindest and politest man and many years later he married Denis and me at Wesley's Chapel in London.
>
> *Source*: Margaret Thatcher, *The Path to Power*, HarperCollins 1995, pp. 10–11.

The Spanish Civil War (1936–39) was very much the litmus test of political response. It divided those Methodists who took any notice of it. Henry Carter, with other leaders, visited Spain in January 1937 at the invitation of the Republicans. Another group, which included Herbert Workman, J. E. Rattenbury and

Anglicans as perceptive as J. K. Mozley and N. P. Williams,[3] were concerned about the 'Red Menace' in Spain, presumably because of Republican persecution of Catholics. In 1936, there was a Conference condemnation of Mussolini for invading Abyssinia, while Leslie Weatherhead had previously suggested Britain might offer territory to Italy! In a sermon, the Cambridge historian, Bernard Lord Manning, was far more prophetic: 'We have seen the triumph of honour without conscience, of militarism without courage, of savagery without ignorance, of science without civilization, of popery without Christianity . . . the venerable lion of Judah has been brought down by the most notorious and most base of ex-socialist journalists.'[4] The ambiguities of all these issues can be pursued in Alan Wilkinson's study *Dissent or Conform?*.

The churches were slow to realize the implications of the rise of Fascism. Few wanted to take on Hitler 'for the sake of people far away of whom we know nothing,' to quote Chamberlain, whom many cheered after Munich. In the last analysis, as we have seen, most faced the inevitability of war. Then most Methodists supported it. Archbishop Lang and other church leaders were 'appeasers' – that is, they simply did not want to go to war. Lang backed the appeasement policy with almost pacifist rhetoric as the will of God; then, as soon as the government declared war, he backed the 'Just War' theory. There are in our period frequent oscillations between non-violence, appeals to the Sermon on the Mount and a rather uncritical espousal of the 'Just War' and 'Just Revolution' theories. A Conference statement in 1957 illustrates the paradox, acknowledging that war is contrary to the spirit, teaching and purpose of our Lord [30].

The 'Just War' theory is set out, with a rejection of nuclear weapons as totally unjust. Nowhere is Erasmus' devastating argument admitted that no one thinks his war is unjust. Nor is it asked 'Who is the just umpire?' It is amazing how readily churches uncritically state 'Just War' theories when it suits them. Methodism is no exception, though in recent years Dr Kenneth Greet has cogently criticized the whole approach in *The Big Sin* (1982).

The war saw the churches in the forefront of progressive thought. William Temple's exclusively Anglican Malvern Conference of 1941 and his *Christianity and Social Order* (1942), with its plea for freedom, fellowship and service as the three principles of a Christian social order, were pointers to a Christian consensus. The organization called the Sword of the Spirit championed by the irenic Cardinal Hinsley, the British Council of Churches in 1942, the backing given to the Welfare State blueprinted by William Beveridge in 1942, and the churches' participation in the Butler Act of 1944 were other symptoms of the new consensus. The dual system of state and church schools no longer aroused Nonconformist wrath – Scott Lidgett was active here as he had been in the controversies of 1902. The strife of a century was largely over, and Archibald Harrison, Principal of Westminster College, articulated a Free Church view which accepted the central place for Religious Instruction (later RK and RE) in all state schools.

Styles of evangelism as in Religion and Life Weeks (the first was in Bristol) and later the Christian Commando Campaigns also reflected wartime progressive consensus. Wilbert Howard pointed to new hopes at the Methodist Conference in 1944 when he was president [31].

The post-war world saw Methodism, despite all the awful trauma of war damage, remarkably vibrant. Lively leaders, ministerial and lay, emerged and, as we shall see, in the decade after the war Methodist scholarship was second to none in the wider church. The World Council of Churches was finally established, with great expectations, at the Amsterdam Conference in 1948, though it was a drawback of the first magnitude that it was unable to include the

---

30. All Christians agree that war is evil. Some believe that it is therefore in every circumstance to be rejected by the followers of Christ. Others believe there are situations in which the waging of war is inevitable as the choice of the lesser of two evils.

*Source*: Statement of the Methodist Conference on *Peace and War* (1957).

31. . . . the overwhelming majority in the Church as well as in the union clearly recognize that in this conflict forced upon the civilized world by a ruthless diabolism there was but one choice to be made. Here stand we. We can no other. So help us GOD! For the sake of the ultimate decencies of life this conflict must be carried through with inflexible resolution until that victory has been won without which there can be no peace . . . We are living in a rapidly changing world and in the realm of thought the true statesman is he who can look ahead and recognize the trend of knowledge and the bearing of remote currents of thought upon the content and presentation of the Christian message. A superficial acquaintance with the jargon of the latest craze may give the impression of modernity but it is a poor sham. We have never lacked the statesmanship of action. I wish that we were better equipped as a Church with the statesmanship of thought.

*Source*: Presidential Address to the Methodist Conference, 1944, reprinted in W. F. Lofthouse et al., *Wilbert F. Howard*, Epworth Press 1954, pp. 42, 48–49.

Roman Catholics, who were the largest Christian group. Methodist involvement has always been wholehearted. Newton Flew of Wesley House, Cambridge, was Chairman of 'Faith and Order', the doctrinal wing of the Council which we will discuss later. Since so often political issues are the only World Council matters featured by the media, the theological work of 'Faith and Order' needs to be kept in mind. The general assemblies at Amsterdam (1948), Evanston (1954), New Delhi (1961) and Nairobi (1975) tackled major theological as well as political themes.

But there was a shift in the style of the World Council. The end of what had been called 'the Vasco da Gama era' had come: the white Anglo-Saxon Protestant West could no longer impose its will, its civilization or its theology on the rest of the world. The Orthodox churches came into the Council, and the initiative began to shift to Asia, Africa, South America. At the General Assembly at Uppsala (1968), following an earlier consultation on 'Christians in the technical and social revolutions of our time' at Geneva in 1966, the new emphases came to the fore. There was a desperate concern for justice as well as peace, for racial equality and for the poor of the world. The Conference almost coincided with the meeting of Roman Catholic bishops at Medellin in Colombia which put forward 'the preferential option for the poor', which has dominated Christian concern over social issues ever since. The same year witnessed both the assassination of Martin Luther King, who had been invited to the Assembly, and widespread student revolts: a world-wide phenomenon, partly deadly serious, partly a passing mood. It was also the year of the Soviet suppression of Czechoslovakia's 'human face of socialism' policy.

So the mood was changing. Professor Michael Howard wrote: 'All but a tiny minority of those who once marched, demonstrated and sat down to ban the bomb, have learned to live with it. Their successors take the balance of terror for granted. They are indeed less concerned with peace than they are with injustice. Whereas ten years ago the pressure was to abolish war at whatever the cost to international order, today it is rather to secure justice at whatever cost to international peace.'[5] A symbol was the creation by the WCC in 1969 of the Programme to Combat Racism (PCR) with its controversial 'Special Fund'. Colin Morris, President of the United Church of Zambia, stated his view of the illegal 'Smith Regime' in Rhodesia which Prime Minister Harold Wilson and Archbishop Michael Ramsey in 1965 thought might have to be suppressed by force [32]. Later Ramsey was dubious about the PCR's support of violent action as, indeed, were the South African churches at first.[6]

Morris's statement stems from desperate concern but crucial issues are raised about the nature of force, violence, national sovereignty, the dangerous concept of a 'war for righteousness' and the role of the churches in politics. Grants were given from the 'Special Fund' of the PCR for humanitarian purposes to most of the African 'freedom fighting' groups in Rhodesia (Zimbabwe after 1980), Angola, Mozambique and Namibia. Despite attempts by the right wing media to do so, no one should impugn the

> **32.** Yes, I believe a Christian is justified in using violence to win freedom in Rhodesia; I know no other way he can get it. I fear innocent women and children will suffer, and I badly want to add 'which, God forbid', but this is a pious subterfuge, inviting the Almighty to stave off the worst consequences of a responsibly-made decision . . . I believe freedom fighters are justified in using any methods short of sadistic cruelty for its own sake to overthrow the Salisbury regime.
>
> It may be a sad thing but in the twentieth century violence is one of the most important mechanisms of social and political change . . . Violence, to put it in Dantean terms, may well not establish a Paradise but it can destroy an Inferno!
>
> *Sources*: Colin Morris, *Unyoung, Uncoloured, Unpoor*, Epworth Press 1969, p. 19; and *Mankind My Church*, Hodder & Stoughton 1971, p. 38.

sincerity or the motives of those who sought to uproot racism and oppression. If theological backing was needed, it came from Barth and Bonhoeffer and the German church struggle against Hitler rather than from Marxism. Nevertheless there was lively debate in Methodism over this matter, especially in 1974 when Conference again approved its grants for the 'Special Fund' by donations from missionary funds. Methodism had always supported the cause of Anti-Apartheid in South Africa, but conflicting attitudes emerged. There were those who espoused pacifism, passive-resistance and non-violent protest, often strangely silent. There were those who were not happy with the apparent partiality of the WCC, which did not appear to apply the same criteria to Soviet oppression of Christian dissidents and Jews. The representatives of the Orthodox Churches played an ambivalent role. Those who raised these points with the WCC secretariat felt that their views were ignored. It is now clear that Africa had become the 'cockpit' of the Second Cold War.

When the Soviet Union collapsed in 1989 and the supply of money and training from the Communist bloc was cut off, the situation changed dramatically. What John de Gruchy has called 'revolution by negotiation' became possible. Was Bush able to reassure President de Klerk of American aid now that the 'soviet factor' was removed from Southern Africa? Nelson Mandela was released in February 1990 after twenty-five years in prison, and the liberation movement was 'unbanned'. Seemingly incredible events began which led to the elections of 1994 when Nelson Mandela became President of South Africa, with de Klerk also involved in the government of a democratic, multi-racial state. The churches can rightly claim much credit here.[7]

Events of history have their own strange momentum and life, a matter recently underlined by the Marxist historian Eric Hobsbawm in a brilliant chapter on Africa in *Age of Extremes: The Short Twentieth Century* (1994) and confirmed from the standpoint of a South African liberation theologian by John de Gruchy in his *Christianity and Democracy* (1995). Both resist any utopian optimism.

Most of the other guerrilla groups have also come to power – Frelimo in Mozambique is a classic case – and have been slowly transformed into semi-ruling parties, now to a large extent dependent on the West. None of that could have been foreseen in 1969. The situation in Rhodesia epitomized the key issues. Opposite is Canaan Banana, Methodist minister and the first President of Zimbabwe, writing after the negotiations under Margaret Thatcher's government in 1979 and the subsequent elections in February 1980 [33].

As far as English Methodism was concerned, the Charity Commissioners directed that gifts to the PCR Special Fund must be the voluntary contributions of individuals, not grants from missionary funds as such. I recall a Latvian lady in Halifax being very relieved because she did not wish any of her money to go to what she called 'Marxist Guerillas'. Her point, as a refugee years ago from Soviet oppression, was serious and proper. Such are the ironies of political theology. The matter was made more difficult by the attitude to Marxism of some Christians, including Methodists. For example, José Miguez Bonino, an Argentinian Methodist and a Vice-President of the WCC, wrote two books expounding liberation theology, in which, incautiously, he commended Cuba and the Soviet

33. The WCC correctly identified the imperatives of these struggles by recognizing that colonialism and foreign domination were inconsistent with the principles of the right of peoples of any country to shape their own independence and to enjoy freedom from colonial domination and exploitation . . . The WCC and the churches cannot assume the authority to determine what methods are proper or improper for the liberation struggles of oppressed people . . . Rather, the question of the forms of the struggle should be left to the struggling peoples themselves. In Zimbabwe the armed struggle was justified by R. G. Mugabe in the statement 'The justice of our causes is our gun'. (Banana goes on to differentiate legitimate struggle from 'anti-liberation mercenary campaigns sponsored by foreign powers as in Mozambique in recent times.')

*Source*: C. Banana art. 'Liberation, Struggles for' in *Dictionary of the Ecumenical Movement* ed. N. Lossky, J. M. Bonino, P. Webb, G. Wainwright and others, WCC, Geneva 1991, pp. 606–7.

Union as models for the future.[8] One is reminded of Sidney and Beatrice Webb in the 1930s, hoodwinked by Stalin and writing of 'a new civilization'. Despite Edward Rogers' fine *Commentary on Communism* (1951) and the realism of the BCC-sponsored *Discretion and Valour* (1974) by Trevor Beeson, some Methodists and others appeared to be persuaded that Marxism–Leninism would triumph in Asia and Africa. Were the writings of storm petrels like Alexander Solzhenitzyn and Andre Sakharov, not to mention the work of Michael Bordeaux at Keston College, downplayed? As Owen Chadwick put it: 'As part of the control of Churches, the States wished to cut or at least weaken the Churches' links with bodies outside the State – the Pope for the Roman Catholics, the Ecumenical Patriarch at Constantinople for the Orthodox and the World Council of Churches for the Protestants. But in this last case, to be inside the World Council was useful, provided that the suitable people were selected or permitted to attend.'[9] We do well to remember how the Russian invasion broke the heart of the fine Czech theologian, Josef Hromadka, who believed that Christianity and Marxism might be reconciled. Despite the ambiguities of the Cold War, no one should denigrate the whole-hearted support given to those fighting oppression and Apartheid. The disputes for most Methodists were not over the motives or the goal but over the methods and the political complexities.

The whole episode of the campaign against Apartheid illustrates the point that Methodist social attitudes have maximum impact when they are shared by other churches. In this campaign, Methodists like Philip Potter, Pauline Webb and David Haslam played a prominent part. Some Methodists, however, will still express concern at the confusing way in which the pendulum swung from pacifism to 'Just War' theories and later back to pacifism and opposition to the Arms Trade. We have learned from these episodes that, as the significant *Political Responsibility* document accepted by the Methodist Conference in 1995 underlined, political responsibility is a complex matter. Prior to this, two reports, *Accept and Resist, a Study of Civil Disobedience Belief in Christian History and To-Day* (1988) and *Sects and Parties: Christian Values and Political Ideologies* (1991), expressed a much more balanced view than that sometimes presented in the 1970s and revealed the great diversity of political views within the church.

## 3. Domestic politics

The 1980s saw Methodism very much concerned with domestic politics in the period dominated by Margaret Thatcher, on whom Dr Alan Wilkinson's Anglican comment is cogent [34].

34. . . . she has brought into contemporary political life, much to the amazement of many of her own party and of the general public, certain aspects of the dissenting heritage which seemed only a few years ago to have gone for ever. The fact that some of her sternest critics have been found among the members of the Free Churches is a measure of how far they have moved away from the spirit of Victorian and Edwardian Nonconformity.

*Source*: A. Wilkinson, *Dissent or Conform?*, SCM Press 1986, p. 82.

Nevertheless British society, as the Brixton riots of 1981 (paralleled in Liverpool and Manchester), the miners' strike and massive unemployment clearly showed, was not at peace with itself. Such unrest cannot be blamed on any one party's policy, but can be seen as signifying the end of the Industrial Revolution. The geographer Peter Hall puts his finger on a key factor. He had cities like Liverpool in mind when he described the dilemma of the inner-city inhabitants. 'A significant minority of the residents are poorly educated, are unskilled, have incomes too low to travel far and perceptions too limited to know the possibilities. They could perform the heavy simple jobs needing much strength but little skill, that once were plentiful. But in the new age of the automated machine and the computer there is no place for their modest talents.'[10] Though bluntly realistic, this analysis may appear to some grossly patronizing. In urban priority areas – whatever the complicated causes – there was higher unemployment than elsewhere, decaying housing, sub-standard educational and medical provision, and social disintegration.

The Methodist Conference protested strongly at policies, such as the Community Charge, which proved to be wrongheaded, but the underlying trends are more important. Out of desperate concerns, some expressed for twenty-five years by Dr John Vincent and the Urban Theology Unit (UTU) in Sheffield and others pressed by the Home Mission Division, there began the project Mission Alongside the Poor. It was launched in 1981 – significantly, well before the much more prestigious Church of England report *Faith in the City* (1985) sponsored by Archbishop Runcie and the subsequent Church Urban Fund (CUF) which, despite somewhat ridiculous denigration by government sources, gave it teeth. Mission Alongside the Poor may be on a smaller scale, but was designed to avoid patronizing the poor by handing out charity. In Bolton, where a century earlier Dr Thomas Bowman Stephenson began his work alongside the poor, Mission Alongside the Poor (supported by CUF) enabled Peter Nazir Ali (an Asian Christian) to act as a community worker in the inner belt, an area where there can be some tension between various strata of a multi-racial community. A UTU work book set out some objectives [35]:

> 35. to explore the divisions of society today, to arouse the Christian conscience about poverty and deprivation, to study the gospel as good news to the poor, to hold up places and activities which represent Christ's mission among the poor, to motivate the whole church to share in the church's mission among the needy in the cities.
>
> *Source: Two Nations, One Gospel*, Urban Theology Unit 1981, p. 2.

A somewhat different but very relevant style is found in documents coming from Luton Industrial College and the Home Mission Division. The pamphlets *Work and Witness* (1977) and the more controversial *Shaping Tomorrow* (1981), which followed up an earlier report on *Industry in Relation to the Social Order* (1960), are typical. The reports reveal both a lively appreciation of the complexities of social change and a way in which the thinking done in Methodism could be shared with other Christians. Such matters, being far beyond the competence of any one denomination, demand ecumenical consideration.

Another important area is the work done by Methodism at many levels to combat racism (in the church as well as outside it) and to enable ethnic groups to secure not only proper equality but also integration with the whole community. The statement *Faithful and Equal* (1987) offers far more than a slogan and is meant to be taken seriously by the whole church.

Finally, we must point to Dr Stephenson's foundation, the National Children's Home (now NCH Action for Children) which is the country's second largest child-care charity with over 200 projects throughout Great Britain and abroad, a staff of 2,700 and an annual budget of £50 million. Over 16,000 children and young people are helped in projects ranging from family centres to alternatives to custody schemes for young offenders and centres for children like that at Edgworth in the Bolton circuit.

Methodism may not be as large a church as it once

was, but its work for human need is large-scale and complex – matter for which the church can take some proper pride.

## For discussion

1. Why do you think the Free Churches have declined in numbers and influence? Why are some Free Churches growing now?
2. How should we get across a personal Christian morality?
3. Have we been right to allow the marriage of divorced people in church and to exercise pastoral caring in this area?
4. Examine the 1976 Statement on Abortion. Does it still stand?
5. Were Christians right to give open support to 'freedom fighters' in Africa? Examine the 'Just War' and 'Just Revolution' theories. Do they still hold water?
6. How should we now help South Africa, especially economically?
7. How should we express political responsibility locally and nationally?

# 5

# The Methodist Emphases Today

Now a change of mood as we do some theology. Why are you a Methodist, Baptist, Anglican or agnostic? Perhaps your mother was one – no bad reason – or perhaps you married one. In my case, my mother was a Methodist, but the fact that the Methodist church up the road had a more attractive youth club than the parish church down the road, where my grandmother was an active worshipper, was another potent factor! Remembering these complexities, let us probe Methodism's theological roots.

Methodism, it is important to stress, has no special doctrines, but its theological orientation is indicated in the Deed of Union [36]. Wisely, no definition of the 'fundamental principles of the Reformation' was offered in 1932, but in 1998 I take the phrase to be shorthand for the sovereignty of God's grace and love, the all-important human response in faith and trust to that love shown in Jesus Christ, the primacy of scripture in establishing doctrine and practice, and the priesthood of all believers. The last phrase – the priesthood of all believers – is open to misunderstanding. It doesn't mean that we are all the same – clearly we are not – or that we all have the same kind of task in the church or the world. What it does mean is that the whole church, every Jack and Jill within it, has a part in the ministry of Christ in prayer, concern, care, witness and sacrifice. No special doctrines, then, but particular emphases or slants, stemming from John Wesley's 'package deal' of Bible, tradition, reason and experience.

---

**36.** (It humbly and proudly) claims and cherishes its place in the Holy Catholic Church which is the Body of Christ. It rejoices in the inheritance of the Apostolic Faith and loyally accepts the fundamental principles of the historic creeds and of the Protestant Reformation.

*Source*: The Deed of Union 1932, *Minutes of the Uniting Conference* 1932, p. 30.

---

The Bible is basic. It is the classic foundation document, like a great signpost pointing to Jesus Christ. If you overstress the Bible, of course, you can end up with a rather wooden biblicism, unconnected with the questions, never contemplated by the biblical writers, which the modern world raises. Nevertheless, the Bible is absolutely indispensable. Without the tradition of the church, however, the living faith of the past, the bread broken from hand to hand for sixty generations, there would be no church at all. Even so, if you overstress tradition, you end up by simply hanging on to the past. The peril of the conservative is complacency, as the peril of the radical is self-righteousness. Faith, therefore, needs to be a contemporary matter, an experienced reality. But if you overstress experience (in a religious sense), you may forget that a 'heart strangely warmed' does not compel you to leave your brains behind when you go to church. It is very easy, if you ignore the conditioning effect of individual temperament, to become too concerned with your religious feelings, or lack of them. In the end, then, the faith has to be thought out and wrestled with. But if you overstress reason you can become too rational, forgetting that we are not 'talking heads' but people with emotions and with two sides to our brains, the logical and the intuitive.

From the 'package deal', then, stem what William B. Fitzgerald in 1903 called the four 'alls' of Methodism. They provide a useful expository framework, even if to some they may seem simplistic because they make no specific reference to vital matters like the incarnation, the church, the sacraments and social responsibility. The four 'alls' – with a fifth added by George Eayrs in 1909 and affirmed by W. E. Sangster in 1951 – are [37]:

---

37. 1. All need to be saved.
    2. All can be saved.
    3. All can know they are saved.
    4. All can be saved to the uttermost.
    5. All must witness to their salvation.

*Source*: *Proceedings of the Eighth Ecumenical Conference*, Epworth Press 1951, p. 73; cf. P. S. Watson, *The Message of the Wesleys*, Epworth Press 1964, p. 35.

---

## 1. All need to be saved

The topic of salvation may remind you of those people who sidle up and ask 'Are you saved?' – and are dumbstruck if you say 'Yes'. It reminds me of a well-heeled lady who bore down on a friend of mine like a Spanish galleon and said, 'Young man, I am not a sinner.' He had been preaching about sin, and she meant, I suppose, that she had done nothing worthy of the attention of 'certain newspapers' and therefore had no need to be saved. As the quotation [38] shows, she was not the first to adopt such an attitude. Not being a sinner and being saved, however, have more to do with the sort of person you are than whose bed you have been in – though, of course, that matters too! Today we are unsure why we need to be saved because we know little about sin, except that, like the preacher, we are supposed to be 'agin' it.

---

38. I thank your ladyship for the information concerning the Methodist preaching. Their doctrines are most repulsive and tinctured with impertinence and disrespect towards their superiors in perpetually endeavouring to level all ranks and do away with all distinctions, as it is monstrous to be told that you have a heart as sinful as the common creatures that crawl the earth. This is highly offensive and insulting.

*Source*: L. Tyerman, *Life of George Whitefield*, London 1890, vol. 1, p. 160. (The Duchess of Buckingham, natural daughter of James II, writing to the Countess of Huntingdon.)

---

The Bible teaches that humanity has a great destiny, that we are made in the image and likeness of God. Unlike sticks or stones or even animals, we are given the capacity for self-consciousness, moral development, self-determination, and fellowship, not as equals but as heirs, with the Creator himself. Indeed, the fact that Jesus Christ was 'born of a woman' shows how closely we share in the creative freedom of God. But humanity is not now in the state intended for it. The book of Genesis tells remarkable stories to help us to tumble to the truth about ourselves. It is more concerned with the nature of sin than with its origins. The story of Adam and Eve – Adam means 'man' and Eve means 'life' – isn't so much about some primaeval ancestors as about you and me. They eat the forbidden fruit, not out of curiosity about sex but to grasp at power. It is an act of rebellion against God. The truth dawns on them when God calls 'Where are you? What are you doing in my world?' Awful guilt follows from that and from the broken human relationships typified by the stories of Cain and Abel (Gen. 4.8–16) and of the Tower of Babel (Gen. 11.1–9). Not only, however, are we responsible for our selfishness, we also feel ourselves to be victims, to be part of an alienated world. In *West Side Story*, that powerful musical, the members of one gang who have murdered the leader of another in a fight meet at a drugstore, boasting of what they have done. The keeper of the store shouts at them, 'You make this world lousy.' 'We found it that way,' is the reply. They feel that they are victims as well as guilty criminals. The Liberation theologians stress, rightly, that sin is corporate as well as individual, that it corrupts states and societies, systems and institutions, as well as you and me. Yet sin is a meaningless word – unlike crime and evil – apart from God. 'Against you, you only, have I sinned' (Ps. 51.4).

This self-assertion works itself out in pride – and first in pride of power. 'Power tends to corrupt' – in the White House, the Kremlin and the village chapel. Sin asserts itself, too, in the pride of knowledge (the idea that there is nothing that human reason cannot do), in the pride which is a perversion of professionalism at all levels ('I know, you don't, so take notice of me') and in the pride of goodness (the self-righteousness in all of us which was the aspect of sin that Jesus could stomach least).

Bishop Lesslie Newbigin[1] recalls a conversation with a member of the team who worked in Chicago on the first atomic bomb. The scientist described the growing excitement as success came nearer and, being ourselves heirs of science and technology, we can imagine how they felt. Then suddenly, when they realized that what they had created was potentially the most monstrous evil that the human mind had devised, their mood changed. They tried desperately to share their anxiety. They wrote to President Truman: 'Try it out in the desert first, please.' No reply! They had created the bomb but 'the system' had taken it out of their hands. There was nothing that they could do to prevent Hiroshima and Nagasaki.

There are many ingredients of the biblical view of sin here. The proper sense of ambition and mastery which can become pride of knowledge, the sense of guilt, the alienation from humankind and nature, the sense of being a victim as well as a responsible human being, the awareness of the future as a mixture of terror and hope – all this, in a word, is what is meant by 'sin'.

Jesus revealed the universality of sin in the Story of The Waiting Father and the Two Brothers (Luke 15.11–32). If the younger brother is a scapegrace, the older brother is full of the pride of goodness. Salvation – all that springs from restored relationships – only came to that house when all three were reconciled. So

sin, fundamentally, is rebellion against God. It is universal, it has its centre in the will, and it produces wrong relationships with God, with fellow human beings and indeed with our environment. It affects all of us – and every part of us – mind and body alike. In the end, we only really see what it is like when we look at the cross of Christ and the events surrounding it. Jesus was not murdered by hooligans on a country road but by the leaders of religion and politics and by the common people who shouted 'Crucify! Crucify!' In other words, a cross-section of humankind took its freedom-bringer, the one who helped people to be real people, and killed him. Though they all thought they were doing good, their action was in reality a challenge to God. But his infinite mercy is big enough to deal with humanity's rebellious self-assertion.

The gospel is a description first of humanity's need, then of the way it can be met. All people need the salvation which is deliverance, restoration, health, wholeness, life of a new quality begun on earth and continued in that eternity where 'we shall know as we are known'. Recovery of health is sometimes a long process – and so is 'being saved'.

## 2. All can be saved

When John Wesley was journeying all over Great Britain, first on his horse, then in a chaise fitted up as a library and a place of work and prayer, there were Christians who thought that only a few, 'the elect', would be saved and, by God's mercy, enter eternal life. We can call these the 'pessimists of grace'. Some of them held a subtle view which enabled them to be successful preachers and evangelists. God, they believed, used preaching to gather in his elect. There were also people – there still are – who thought that, given education, the use of reason and freedom from superstition, humankind was perfectible. A new world, they held, could come by human effort, and there was no limit to progress. We can call these people the 'optimists of nature'.

Wesley, who had no illusions about human nature, believed in original sin. But he also believed that God's love was as universal as human rebellion. God's grace, he affirmed, has always gone before us and never ceases working in the human heart. Wesley was, in short, an 'optimist of grace' – a phrase we shall meet again later – and his understanding of the gospel had a universal note. 'Pure universal love thou art' (*Hymns and Psalms* 434), and therefore no one is beyond the reach of the gospel.

Some of the implications of this view need to be spelled out. Think, for a moment, how our relationships with one another differ from our relationship with God. Our contacts with many of our fellows are formal and functional: we pay tradespeople, for example, for services rendered without entering into a deep and lasting relationship. On the other hand, mutual attraction, affection and respect can lead to friendship and even to marriage. But our relationship with God is different from both cases: it does not depend on any service we render him, and his love is different in kind: 'Love to the loveless shown/that we might lovely be' (*Hymns and Psalms* 173).

Behind any thought of God's love is the centrality of the cross of Christ, that amazing compressed symbol of all that love means. Somehow God does for us what we cannot do for ourselves. He bridges the gulf between himself and us by sharing in the glory of his creation to the full. He enables us to be reconciled to himself, whoever we are. Frances Young [39] spells out what was involved.

---

39. In the end Jesus did not waft away the darkness of the world, all its sin and suffering and hurt and evil, with a magic wand. He entered right into it, took it upon himself, bore it, and in the process turned it into glory, transformed it . . . [A] properly Christian response to the problem of evil has to begin with the cross, with an understanding of atonement. We do not begin by explaining evil away, justifying God, excusing him of the mess he has made of his creation. We begin by contemplating the story which tells of God taking responsibility for the evil in his world by entering it himself, taking it upon himself, in all its horror, cruelty and pain.

*Source*: Frances Young, *Face to Face*, Epworth Press 1985, p. 58.

---

Having begun with God's amazing grace, we go on to our response. We can refuse the love of God. But when, gripped by the 'wonder why such love to me', we respond, what is happening? The Dutch theologian Arminius (1560–1609), who indirectly had a great influence on the Wesleys, tells of a rich man giving alms to the poor and famished beggar, who needs to maintain himself and his family. Does it cease to be a pure gift, he asks, because the beggar stretches out his hand to receive it? John Wesley, like Paul and Martin Luther before him, went further, stressing – as we have seen – the priority of grace in the whole process: pardon on God's side, trust on our side, and all of it pure gift.

Now the brothers John and Charles Wesley, though very conscientious, very religious and very concerned about themselves, did not break through the 'faith barrier' until their early thirties. In February 1738, Charles Wesley was very ill. He was visited by a Moravian called Peter Böhler, one of those irritating people who read our minds and hearts. 'For what reason,' he asked Charles, 'do you hope to be saved?' 'Because I have used my best endeavours to serve God,' was the answer. Böhler shook his head sadly, and Charles records his own reaction: 'What, are not my endeavours a sufficient ground of hope? Would he rob me of my endeavours? I have nothing else to trust to.'[2]

Many, like Charles, still think they need credit in the Building Society in the Sky! To realize that God's love was what really mattered was, for him, like crashing through the sound barrier. 'Faith' is a slippery word. We recall the boy who described it as 'believing what you know ain't true', or the Duchess in *Through the Looking Glass* who said, 'I can believe six impossible things before breakfast. You only need practice.' In our world, it is surprising what folk will believe. Someone offers you a lift, and you put your life in his hands, believing that it will be safe. On holiday in Switzerland, you trust the people who make and maintain the cable cars in which you travel. You get married, and put your trust, your faith, in your partner. Faith in the Christian sense is not a blind date with an unknown God but personal trust in the God who, in Christ, entrusts himself to us and uses the whole of human relationships to open our eyes to God's will.

Faith can be kindled in all sorts of ways. Tertullian (*c.* 160–220), a lawyer, was deeply moved by the demeanour of Christians prosecuted in his court for not giving the customary pinch of incense to the Emperor's statue. What made these people tick? 'The blood of martyrs is seed,' he said; and he was part of the crop. A man in my congregation was not clear what he believed. One day at a baptism, when the congregation made its vow to be a true fellowship of caring, he realized that he wanted to be part of it. Faith is trust in the person of Jesus, in whom we see divine love and human trust and obedience bound up together. Mind, feeling and will are engaged in response to him. If you find faith and trust in God difficult – as, if we are honest, we all do sometimes – remember Oliver Cromwell, who said to his daughter, Bridget: 'To be a seeker is to be of the next best sect to a finder, and such a one shall every faithful seeker be at the end.' Gonville ffrench Beytagh, when in gaol for his opposition to Apartheid, described how he came to the heart of the matter: 'Salvation, I believe, is knowing that by myself I am hopeless and helpless and that if I want to be accepted, God accepts me.'[3] Perhaps his situation was uniquely helpful in revealing the heart of Paul's doctrine by justification by faith. The condition of salvation is faith, faith from start to finish.

From this starting point derives not the idea 'I'm saved – it doesn't matter what I do now,' but a whole pattern of life expressing love for others. Somehow a final verdict – 'Forgiven!' – has been given. The situation is like a slaver telling a slave 'You're free!'; like a judge declaring 'Acquitted!'; like a new family saying 'Welcome!' We don't have to worry about our credit with God. If God vindicates us, we stand for others. Christian ethics, in short, is based on gratitude and works by love. We dare, as Martin Luther put it, to be 'Christ to our neighbour'.

You may have heard about John Wesley's 'warmed heart'. We all need to recall what warmed it. It was hearing the reading [40] from Martin Luther.

> 40. . . . the Spirit makes the heart glad and free as the law requires that it shall be. Faith, however, is a divine work in us. It changes us and makes us to be born anew of God . . . O it is a living, busy, active, mighty thing, this faith, and so it is impossible for it not to do good works incessantly . . . Faith is a living, daring, confidence in God's grace, so sure and certain that a man would stake his life on it a thousand times. This confidence in God's grace, and the knowledge of it, makes a man glad and bold and happy in dealing with God and with all his creatures; and this is the work of the Holy Ghost in faith. Hence a man is ready and glad, without compulsion, to do good to everyone, to serve everyone, to suffer everything, in love and praise of God, who had shown him this grace; and thus it is impossible to separate works from faith, as impossible as to separate heat and light from fire.
>
> *Source*: *Works of Martin Luther*, Philadelphia, Pa. 1932 VI, pp. 449f.

Anyone put right by faith is really part of a new world – the experience is like being born all over again – and lives authentically by giving themselves for Christ and others. This is very different from whipping ourselves into frantic 'do-gooding'. To underline the implications, Colin Morris, missionary in Zambia, later President of the Methodist Conference, puts the matter graphically: 'It is justified man who engages in the struggle for justice . . . no escape there. It is the motive that matters. It is reconciled man who seeks to end conflict, reborn people who work to bring forth a newer, safer society.'[4] Maybe the greatest contribution of Methodism is a grasp of that great wholeness of being which begins and ends in Christ. The haunting words of Sir Herbert Butterfield [41] put the same kind of conviction in a different way.

> 41. There are times when we can never meet the future with sufficient elasticity of mind, especially if we are locked in the contemporary systems of thought. We can do worse than remember a principle which both gives us a firm Rock and leaves us the maximum elasticity for our minds: the principle: Hold fast to Christ, and for the rest be totally uncommitted.
>
> *Source*: H. Butterfield, *Christianity and History*, Bell 1949, p. 146.

## 3. All can know they are saved

Can they? This is an area where we need great sensitivity. Genuine assurance of what God has done for us in Christ is an important factor in our Christian life and in our impact on others. Indeed, one Christian philosopher, H. D. Lewis, goes so far as to say 'the core of religion is religious experience', a view commonplace enough among Methodist scholars in the 1920s and 1930s. Few things are more harmful, however, than the smug religious complacency which ignores or spurns the doubts and fears of those who, for all sorts of temperamental and intellectual reasons, find such religiosity off-putting, preferring more modest modes of religious life-style and communication. It is probable that, in recent times, not a few people in Methodism have been made to feel guilty because their spiritual pilgrimage has been different from that of the Wesleys and some of their followers. We need to recall both that the Wesleys were extraordinary, not least in their parents, and that John Wesley's heart was warmed by a preface to a theological commentary on the most searching of Paul's letters. It was, in short, theology that brought him to the assurance of faith.

If we make our experience a cause for vanity or boasting, we are condemned. But if the gospel is believed, it must, by its very nature, stir us in the depths of our being. To enjoy our emotions, however, is not necessarily part of, and may well be a hindrance to, our total response to God in thought, feeling and will.

The only doctrine of assurance which has any firm basis in the New Testament is one rooted in the work of the Holy Spirit. 'The witness of the Spirit' is indeed the best term for it. Only a church which is constantly and profoundly conscious of the Spirit's activity can really talk about assurance without encouraging the deadly sin of pride or self-centredness. It is the Spirit who always points to Christ and makes his person and work contemporary to us. It is the Spirit who enables us to say 'Jesus is Lord.' It is the Spirit who enables us to call God our Father, and to say 'This is our Father's world.' This was the heart of the experience of Jesus

himself who, in this sense, was 'charismatic'. Our assurance is grounded in what happened at Calvary and on Easter Day. This is the assurance of God's pardon and of a relationship restored, not an assurance that we are worthy or at least 'no small beer' in God's sight. Even John Wesley fell into a trap here. For some time, he and his preachers asserted that, unless a person had a conscious assurance of salvation, they were simply not pardoned by God. As this passage [42] makes clear, he came later to see that this was an extravagant view. John Fletcher, Vicar of Madeley, a saint if ever there was one, expressed a properly Methodist view when he said, 'I build not on my experience, though this increases, but on the revealed truth of God.'

---

42. When fifty years ago my brother Charles and I in the simplicity of our hearts told the good people of England that unless they knew their sins forgiven they were under the wrath and curse of God I marvel they did not stone us. The Methodist I hope now knows better. We preach assurance as we always did as a common privilege of the people of God but we do not enforce it under the pain of damnation.

*Source*: Melville Horne, *An Investigation to the Definition of Justifying Faith*, Longman 1809, pp. 1–4; 7–10; 12, 14. (An account of a conversation with John Wesley.)

---

But what of Christians who simply do not appear to have intense religious experiences? Is Methodism not for them? What of those Christians who speak of the 'dark night of the soul' as of a tunnel without even a glimpse of light at the end of it, or those for whom talk of the purgative, illuminative and unitary way expresses the Christian pilgrimage more realistically than stress on 'peak experiences'? In the end, we can only underline that we have assurance because of what Christ has done for us. Martin Luther, when depression was on him – Winston Churchill called it the 'black dog', and some of us know what that means – used to cry out, 'I have been baptized.' He thus affirmed that Christ had put his hand on him and would never let him go. Kingsley Barrett [43] puts the matter very well.

---

**43.** If you can stomach the old-fashioned word, it is a matter of assurance, assurance that is rooted not in my personal self-confidence but precisely in that which is not I. The hand with which I hold God is a trembling hand indeed, but the hand with which he holds me will never let me go, and in that confidence, that assurance, I can and must preach as dying man to dying men; and this I cannot do unmoved.

*Source*: Address to the Methodist Conference, *Epworth Review* January 1974, pp. 106–7.

---

It may be helpful to make a distinction between 'certainty' and 'certitude'. You can have a reasonable 'certainty' about a mathematical proposition or the colour of your husband's eyes but not about a personal relationship. Here the highest we can reach is 'certitude', based on trust. And the same is true of faith: there is a 'certitude' within the gracious personal relationship which God offers us.

That wise old man von Staupitz told the young Martin Luther, when he was looking for 'certainty' in matters of faith, that he should 'begin with the wounds of Jesus'. For some this may sound like 'language of Zion' which simply does not 'click' any more. So let's try another tack. Some modern Roman Catholic writers speak of the 'Second Journey'. We all go through the 'First Journey' – birth, home, school, adolescence, the quest for personal identity, followed by college or work or, sadly, the dole. Quite often, religious commitment comes naturally during this journey. It came to John Wesley in 1725 when he devoted himself entirely to God, and he later called it 'the faith of a servant'. At a later stage, deep relationships leading to marriage may be formed or perhaps the realization dawns that being single can be creative, not least in the church. The 'First Journey', in other words, can be long and satisfying. But it can also come to an abrupt halt. The death of a partner, or the loss of a job, or even divorce can cause the question 'Who am

I?' to rush at us again. In John Wesley's case, it was failure in Georgia and a broken love affair which helped to move him from 'the faith of a servant' ('What can I do for God?') to 'the faith of a son' ('What can Christ do with me?'). The assurance which came on 24 May 1738 at the meeting in Aldersgate Street enabled Wesley to proceed, tentatively, towards the goal of 'perfect love'. Was his experience, we may ask, what those influenced by the Charismatic Movement call 'Baptism of the Spirit' – a peak experience coming after conversion and bringing what I have called 'certitude', and with it new power and creativity, new gifts and insights for a 'Second Journey'?

## 4. All can be saved to the uttermost

John Wesley [44] indicated what Methodism's constant doctrines are by using the analogy of a house.

---

**44.** I have again and again, with all the plainness I could, declared what our constant doctrines are, whereby we are distinguished only from heathens or nominal Christians, not from any that worship God in spirit and in truth. Our main doctrines, which include all the rest, are three – that of Repentence, of Faith, and of Holiness. The first of these we account, as it were, the porch of religion; the next, the door; the third, religion itself.

*Source*: John Wesley, *Letters*, Standard Edition Vol. II, pp. 267–68.

---

Holiness, then, was for Wesley 'religion itself' and he often referred to it as 'perfect love'. The goal of the Christian life, in other words, is not something achievable by an isolated individual, as theoretically 'perfect faith' might be, but something that binds the believer to others. As Wesley himself said, 'there is no holiness but social holiness'. How then is such holiness acquired or, to put it another way, how is such a capacity to love God and neighbour developed? As Frederic Greeves points out [45], this is where the church comes in.

> 45. A community worshipping, thinking, working to-
> gether, bound together by the fellowship of the Holy
> Spirit in a common love for God and for His Son so that
> the stronger help the weaker and the older aid the
> younger in the craft of Christian love – that is the true
> church . . . In such a church 'full salvation' is no mere
> pious phrase, and holiness no utopian and somewhat
> frightening ideal. And when Christians learn to love with
> a love like Christ's, other people want more readily to
> become Christian.
>
> *Source*: F. Greeves, *Theology and the Cure of Souls*,
> Epworth Press 1960, pp. 78–79.

Within the Methodist church, the contribution of small groups – whether known as 'classes' or 'bands' or 'house groups' – has been appreciated from the first. They are places where experience of worship, prayer and searching of the scriptures can promote spiritual growth. They are also places where individuals find challenge, acceptance and healing in the fullest sense. We need therefore to ask about our churches: Are they communities where, in such groups, people can grow and mature or do they stunt and maim people and leave them immature? Indeed, since the South American 'basic communities' are teaching us that true fellowship is sharing in the Holy Spirit, we need to ask whether we can discern in our churches the fruit or harvest of the Spirit.

The fourth 'all', then, points to the goal of the Christian life, perfect love for God himself and for others. The early Methodist view of this has been called an 'optimism of grace' because, while it has no illusions about human nature, it puts no limits to what God, in his gracious relationship with us, can do.

At the same time, such holiness is meant to flow into the whole of life and, while Wesley believed in transformation, he never adequately worked the matter out. R. W. Dale, the famous Congregationalist preacher and theologian, was therefore right to complain at the end of the last century that Methodism had never really developed the doctrine of Christian perfection beyond the sphere of individual spirituality. In the twentieth century, however, Methodists have recognized that love is needed in every facet of life. As Dag Hammarskjøld said, 'the path to holiness is of necessity followed in our times by the taking of action'.[5] The Christian therefore working in the Health Service, seeking a cure for AIDS or MS, striving through the UN for reconciliation among nations, attempting in a trade union to see complex social issues in a Christian perspective or making a home for spouse and children can be working out what perfect love may mean in today's world.

Perhaps Methodism has been successful in promoting personal integrity, on the one hand, and a deep concern for world issues, on the other, but less good in the middle area where the imperatives of the gospel can be appallingly difficult to put into practice. I recall a Christian manager, who had to sack workers to save his firm, asking, 'What does the Christian ethic say to me now?'

We fulfil the law of love only in so far as, in specific situations, we are concerned to enable folk to see some purpose in living, whether that person happens to be the woman sitting next to you in the choir whom you don't like very much, or the young woman in your office mixed up about her boyfriend, or the old lady next door who is 'shut in' and hardly has a caller, or the little boy dying of leukaemia because, perhaps, we have fouled God's creation with unnecessary radiation. The fearful dangers in such situations are a feeling of hopelessness or a somewhat self-righteous obsession. It was said of Mother Teresa, that very practical saint: 'The poor deserve not just service and dedication but also the joy that belongs to human love. Their greatest need of all is to be wanted, valued, cared for, loved. And if they should die, then she will move heaven and earth to let them die with the sight of a loving face.'[6]

Against this background, then, we can see why John Wesley claimed that the doctrine of Christian perfection was the 'grand depositum' which God had lodged with the Methodists and wanted them to share with others. We can also begin to understand why W. E. Sangster, when President of the Methodist Conference in 1951, constantly stressed that the greatest need of the church was 'saints' – ordinary folk, made extraordinary by grace, who by their love of God and neighbour make it easier for others to believe.

Some people, however, may still wonder whether, despite the saints, perfection or 'perfect love' is possible this side of the grave. The perfectly loving person, of course, will not realize what they are. And John Wesley was wise not to claim Christian perfection for himself, since he was at times imperious and lacking in sensitivity. But the basic question concerns the character of Christian life and the way in which grace works within it. The very existence of 'peak experiences' and the prevalence of talk about the 'Second Journey' points to the fact that the Christian life is not like a steadily moving escalator from womb to tomb. It is often a series of jumps, each followed by steady progress. Just as, in a marriage, relationships can suddenly deepen and be strangely enriched by bereavement or illness or crises faced together, so our Christian discipleship can be marked by 'peak experiences' which open our lives to God and illuminate the rest of our pilgrim way. John Wesley stressed both the moment by moment relationship and what his brother Charles liked to call the 'great salvation'.

We do well, then, to thank God for flashes of his glory, gifts of his grace, and then press on. We have no need to waste emotional energy agonizing about whether we have reached the goal of 'perfect love' or not. We simply believe the maximum.

Finish then thy new creation,
    Pure and spotless let us be;
Let us see thy great salvation,
    Perfectly restored in thee:
Changed from glory into glory,
    Till in heaven we take our place,
Till we cast our crowns before thee,
    Lost in wonder, love, and praise!
*(Hymns and Psalms 267)*

## For discussion

1. Is it sectarian to have special emphases? Do other Christians think it rather 'odd'? Especially when we are always bringing up John Wesley.

2. How did you come to a Methodist or other church? How have you developed your faith since? What have been the drawbacks?

3. Does the doctrine of justification by faith so stressed by the Reformers ring any bells now? Have we failed to put it in modern terms?

4. Is assurance a dangerous idea? Why? How is it that some people have such a clear religious confidence while others do not? What is the place of religious experience?

5. 'Christian Perfection! How horrid' said a German lady to me once. Is this an impossible idea? How do members of other Christian Communions express it?

6. What of the means of grace? Do we find they help us to move on to maturity?

7. What really matters – personal holiness or social responsibility or both?

# 6

# Methodist Worship
# and Preaching

Anglican and Free Church people are often puzzled by Methodist worship. If, on the one hand, they attend a 'preaching service', they find little different from the worship of the average Baptist or United Reformed Church: hymns and songs, extempore prayer (wholly spontaneous or prepared for the occasion or taken from a book) and a sermon, frequently linked – in harmony with classic Reformed tradition and recent liturgical thinking – with set readings. They may or may not notice that the hymns are carefully chosen and that one, at least, is likely to be by Charles Wesley. The sermon, one hopes, will be a proclamation of the word and not a mere moral exhortation. If, on the other hand, they attend a Methodist communion service, they discover that the Sunday Service (1975) is very like the orders in the Anglican Alternative Service Book (1980), especially in its liturgical shape. In other words, Methodist worship seems to have a mixed pedigree which merits explanation.

There is, moreover, another style of worship which our Anglican and Free Church visitors may encounter in a Methodist church. Among the well-informed, it is called 'All-Age Worship', but in Lancashire we still call it 'Family Worship'! Alongside the adult congregation, members of uniformed organizations may well be present as well as the Junior Church. There is likely to be a great deal of congregational participation, not least through the use of modern hymns and songs, often accompanied by piano, guitars and flutes, and the sermon or demonstration will be geared to the

younger age group but meant for all. Done well, it can be a rich act of worship; done badly, it can be a disastrous travesty. The reasons for the development of this style must also be explored.

## 1. Origins

So some history first. To understand Methodist contributions to worship, we need first to acknowledge the influence of the Anglican tradition of Thomas Cranmer with the Book of Common Prayer revised in 1662 as normative. We need also to recognize significant changes in eighteenth-century English Nonconformity. For although Wesley was never a dissenter, the newer styles of worship, and not least the use of hymns as distinct from metrical psalms, indirectly influenced Methodism. Isaac Watts (1674–1748), whose 'When I survey the wondrous cross' is often said to be the greatest English passion hymn, was a key figure. It was Philip Doddridge (1702–51), however, whose hymns for particular occasions specifically influenced Charles Wesley (1707–88). Indeed, he began to write secular poetry for every possible occasion, including a child having a tooth out before anaesthetics and his cat fighting the 'tom' next door!

John Wesley laid great stress on the 'means of grace' – signs or words or actions ordained by God and appointed for this end: 'to be the ordinary channels whereby he might convey to people prevenient, justifying and sanctifying grace'. The 'means' are prayer, private and public, searching the scriptures, the Lord's Supper, fasting (on Fridays!) and 'Christian Conference', that is, meetings with fellow Christians. To these 'instituted means', he added 'prudential means', i.e. sharing in styles of worship good in themselves (e.g. meeting in 'class', Lovefeasts and Watchnight services, which we will discuss later) and doing works of mercy. So how did all this work out?

The keen Methodist was supposed to go to the parish church, sharing every Sunday in Morning Prayer, the Litany and the first part of the Communion Service (the Ante-Communion) and monthly, or even less frequently in rural parts, in Holy Communion itself. Such, certainly, was Wesley's desire but things did not always turn out as he wished. Some Methodists were not welcome at the parish church, and others felt out of place there, sometimes due to the poor quality of the clergyman or for social reasons of class and dress. The 'societies,' as the Methodist groups were called, would meet each week: on a Sunday, sometimes at 5 am (which was not as extraordinary as it seems to us) and in the late afternoon, and during the week too. Thus the 'preaching service' [46] developed. Its origins are obscure – perhaps one was the 'university sermon,' familiar to Wesley, with prayer, probably a metrical psalm, and a sermon. The late mediaeval 'prone', a vernacular section of the mass, combining sermon and prayers, is also a possible source. Moreover, the dissenting services of psalms (or hymns), readings, sermons and prayers must have been well known to the early Methodists as an alternative to the parish church. Not all the early Methodists had an Anglican background. Features of the preaching service were extempore prayer and hymns by Charles Wesley, 'lined out' by the preacher and thus effectively learned by heart by members of the society. This was an oral tradition of very great importance. The preaching would normally be exposition of scripture, though at first the Bible was not always formally read, perhaps because those present should have heard scripture at Morning Prayer. Wesley's 'assistants' and 'helpers' tried valiantly to emulate the 'offering of Christ' which was the heart of the preaching.

46. (a) If it were designed to be instead of Church service, it would be essentially defective. For it seldom has the four grand parts of public prayer; deprecation, petition, intercession and thanksgiving. Neither is it, even on the Lord's Day, concluded with the Lord's Supper. The hour for it on that day, unless there is some peculiar reason for a variation, should be five in the morning, as well as five in the evening. Why should we make God's day the shortest of the seven?
(b) From the beginning men and women sat apart, as they always did in the Primitive Church; and none were suffered to call any place their own but the first comers sat down first. They had no pews; and all the benches for rich and poor were of the same construction. Mr Wesley began the service with a short prayer; then sung a hymn and preached (usually about half an hour); then sang a few verses of another hymn, and concluded by prayer. His constant doctrine was, salvation by faith, preceded by repentance, and followed by holiness.

*Source*: (a) *Minutes of Conference 1766*, 1862 Edition, Vol. I p. 59; (b) Preaching Service at the Foundery, J. Wesley, *Works*, Jackson Edition 1856, Vol. XIII, p. 245.

We cannot exaggerate the role of Charles Wesley's hymns intended for the society meeting. They both outlined a Christian's spiritual biography and provided devotional material for every kind of occasion. Many, and especially those relating to the Christian year, have been taken up by other denominations: hymns like 'Come, thou long-expected Jesus' (*Hymns and Psalms* = HP 81), 'Hark! The herald angels sing' (HP 106), 'Christ the Lord is risen today' (HP 193), 'Rejoice, the Lord is King!' (HP 243), 'O Thou who camest from above' (HP 745). The 'occasions' include all the new Methodist services – the Lovefeast, the Watchnight, the Covenant Service, for every group will produce its own feasts and fasts. After 1780 Methodism always had an official hymn book which Wesley insisted should normally be used, for he believed that sound doctrine was important and was conveyed in hymnody. 'I care not who makes the nation's laws so long as I could make their ballads.' If the sociologist David Martin is right and 'the hymn is the most central item in the religion of Britain,'[1] then we will do well to reflect on the effect of singing their theology on generations of the Methodists. Hymns were lined out and learned by heart, and thanks to the 'drip feed' of the corpus of Wesley hymns, no group of Christians, over the generations, has carried so much theology in their hearts and heads as the Methodists [47]. Moreover, to underline another Methodist characteristic which is now sadly neglected, I possess my Welsh grandfather's hymn book, black with use in private prayer.

Wesley also translated hymns from the German and used the work of Isaac Watts and versions of the English poets like George Herbert (1593–1633) whose poems – for example, 'Teach me, my God and King' (HP 803) and 'Let all the world in every corner sing' (HP 10) – were never written as hymns but are still used as such.

---

47. You talk much, and you talk rightly, of the work Methodism does for the world and for the universal church; but your greatest – incomparably your greatest – contribution to the common heritage of Christendom is in Wesley's hymns . . . and unless you preserve it for the use of the faithful, till that day when we are all one, we shall all lose some of the best gifts of God.

*Source*: Bernard L. Manning, *The Hymns of Wesley and Watts*, Epworth Press 1942, reissued 1988, p. 13. (Manning was a Cambridge historian, a Congregationalist layman.)

---

A brief look is needed at some of the 'prudential' means of grace. The Lovefeast came from the Moravians and ultimately from the early church's *agape*. Water drunk from a Lovefeast cup and cake (for which there are recipes) were the elements, and hymns were sung, prayer spontaneously offered and testimonies given. In ecumenical circles the *agape* – in rather more restrained form – has had something of a revival in recent years, though to some it appears a way of dodging the pain of not being able to communicate with Roman Catholics. The Watchnight was also Moravian, with an echo of early church 'vigils'. It

was often held on a Friday near to the full moon. The Covenant Service – borrowed from a late Puritan source composed by Richard and Joseph Alleine – began to be regularly used after 1755. It was a very intense form of personal and corporate devotion. It became customary to use it on the first Sunday of the New Year, normally in the afternoon. This was still the case in the 1950s and, for a service of the deeply committed, the timing is just as appropriate today. Its form, however, has changed over the years. The 1936 Book of Offices contained a service based as much on G. B. Robson as on the Alleines. This was revised in 1975 [48] and forms of it can be found in the Book of Common Order of the Church of South India (1962) and in the Book of Common Order of the Church of Scotland (1994).

---

48. I am no longer my own, but yours. Put me to what you will, rank me with whom you will; put me to doing, put me to suffering; let me be employed for you or laid aside for you; exalted for you, or brought low for you; let me be full, let me be empty; let me have all things, let me have nothing; I freely and heartily yield all things to your pleasure and disposal. And now, glorious and blessed God, Father, Son, and Holy Spirit, you are mine and I am yours. So be it. And the Covenant now made on earth, let it be ratified in heaven. Amen.

*Source*: The Covenant Service, *Methodist Service Book*, 1975.

---

Modern criticisms of the Covenant Service[2] have suggested that the eucharist fulfils the same function, that it is not really corporate but individualistic and that baptism is a once and for all covenant. The 1975 form of the service avoids the heart of these criticisms. It is clear that it is a renewal of the Covenant, similar to a renewal of baptismal vows in other churches. It has proved and is proving to be a genuine Methodist/ Puritan contribution to ecumenical worship, recalling God's perpetual covenant with his people, renewed in Christ.

Another 'prudential' means was private prayer and meetings for prayer. All these early meetings took place firstly in private property, often after a preaching service. Later they were held in the purpose-built and formally registered 'meeting houses' which were a tangible sign of a gradual development into a denomination. A Methodist characteristic was the use of lay people as preachers. Some were full-time and, after Wesley's death, evolved into the Wesleyan ministry. Others, the forerunners of Local Preachers, were wholly lay and included some women. Women's preaching faded out after Wesley's death, but was revived among Primitive Methodists (1811) and the Bible Christians (1815), who were also pioneers in having female itinerant preachers, who were often remarkably young.

For the earliest Methodists, Holy Communion would be provided by the parish church but also by Wesley or one of his clerical helpers. Wesley never permitted lay people to preside. Communion services were frequent in London and Bristol which were centres of Methodism. We must not exaggerate the place of the sacraments in early Methodism, for 'Methodism was a sacramental revival in the minds of its leaders'.[3] Very large numbers attended Wesley's eucharists, sometimes in hired buildings like French chapels. The liturgy of the Book of Common Prayer (1662), with the addition of extempore prayer and hymns, was used [49], the service becoming in this way an evangelistic and 'converting' ordinance. A characteristic which has remained is for the congregation to go up to the Holy Table in groups rather than as individuals. The precise origin of this distinctive Methodist custom is unknown. We need to remember also that in the early days a 'class ticket' was normally necessary to attend all meetings of the Methodist society. The communion table open 'to all who love the Lord' is a comparatively modern innovation. It never occurred in any rubrics of the various Methodist groups.

Yet for use in America Wesley amended the Prayer Book order for Holy Communion in what might be considered a Puritan direction. Occasions of the Christian year, though not the principal ones, were omitted. Many psalms were also left out as 'being highly improper in the mouths of a Christian congregation,' and this practice has continued in Methodist hymnbooks, including *Hymns and Psalms* (1983). The word 'priest' was replaced by 'minister' or 'elder' and reference to the baptismal regeneration of infants disappeared, as did godparents and the sign of the cross – all changes reminiscent of the demands of moderate Puritans a century before.

This order of Holy Communion, further modified, was intended for use in Britain too, but in practice the Prayer Book order was still often followed both for Holy Communion and for Morning Prayer. The use of the lectionary was specifically stipulated, but Conference statements often mask widespread ignoring of regulations. So prayer in Methodist worship has been influenced by the corporate, responsive style of the Book of Common Prayer and by the extempore style derived from Puritanism. After Wesley's death the Plan of Pacification of 1795 allowed itinerant preachers to preside at Holy Communion, if the society so

---

**49.** (i) In 1784 John Wesley wrote to the American Methodists:
And I have prepared a Liturgy little differing from that of the Church of England (I think, the best constituted National Church in the world), which I advise all the travelling preachers to use on the Lord's Day in all the congregations, reading the Litany only on Wednesdays and Fridays and praying extempore on all other days. I also advise the elders to administer the Supper of the Lord on every Lord's Day.

*Source*: Letter, 10 September 1780, to 'Our brethren in America,' J. Wesley, *Letters*, Standard Edition Vol. VII, p. 239.

(ii) In a preface, John Wesley added:
I do believe there is no liturgy in the world either in ancient or modern language which breathes more of solid, scriptural, rational piety than the Common Prayer of the Church of England and, though the main part of it was compiled more than 200 years ago, yet is the language of it not only pure but strong and elegant in the highest degree.

*Source*: *The Sunday Service*, 1784.

wished, and after 1805, because evening worship was facilitated by the widespread use of gas lighting, Holy Communion became, for the most part, an evening rite after a preaching service. As time went by, much of Wesley's particular conception was lost, and many of his brother's eucharistic hymns were no longer used.

## 2. Later influences

Wesley clearly moulded Methodist worship, but the frontier tradition of America was also influential, in the USA and later in Britain. Revivalist preaching and camp meetings, with the clear intention of winning converts and often lasting several days, were important. Their style was more 'folksy' than that of John Wesley's field preaching, though the influence of field preaching was always a factor, giving a sense that a service in chapel was an outdoor meeting with a roof on! New styles of hymnody were to be found in Primitive Methodism. American hymns, some of them Methodist, came across the Atlantic, and two styles were soon present in Methodist worship, the Wesley classics being supplemented by the new revival hymns. The latter ranged from Lorenzo Dow's hymns to Frances Jane Van Alstyne's and those later called 'Sankey's', though Sankey only provided the tunes. In our day hymns associated with the Billy Graham missions and later 'worship songs' are in the same tradition of popular hymnody, as indeed were Cliff College choruses.

The worship accompanying the revivalist style of preaching had its own characteristic shape: the sermon provided a final climax and was followed by prayer meetings, counselling of converts or holy communion. In Victorian Methodism this pattern coexisted, in the large town chapels, with a more Anglican style, Morning Prayer being balanced with an evening Free Church style of service. This pattern continued in some places (e.g. Park St, Bolton; Trinity, Wolverhampton; St John's, Sunderland) until at least the 1960s. In some churches, where Morning Prayer was not used, the major canticles would nevertheless be sung and local service books followed. Brunswick, Leeds, and King Cross, Halifax, together with George St, Burton upon Trent, a church in the United Methodist Free Church tradition, provide typical examples.

The Victorian age saw greater assimilation, too, to the ethos of the Free Churches. The principal act of worship became a full-blown service of the word with four or five hymns, prayers, and scripture readings from both Testaments. It offered sermons with a greater attractiveness for the 'adherents', who now outnumbered members in evening worship. Preaching had a more popular appeal, and all the tricks of oratory were copied from exemplars like Morley Punshon. The Victorian preaching service was very different from Wesley's model. Musicians' benches became choirs, organs were installed, and more elaborate buildings had great central pulpits or rostrums.

In 1882 a New Service Book in Wesleyanism maintained the Anglican style Communion service, though with the 'manual acts' – that is, the breaking of bread and the raising of the cup – omitted. The rite of baptism was changed to eliminate any suggestion of baptismal regeneration, despite the writings of the greatest Wesleyan theologian at the time, William Burt Pope. The United Methodist Free Churches, the Primitive Methodists and the Bible Christians all had service books by the end of the century, and the United Methodist Church soon followed. Such books were used for weddings and funerals, and provided a norm for covenant, baptism, and Holy Communion. The Oxford Movement in Anglicanism, with its liturgical, ceremonial and architectural renewal, had an ambivalent effect. There was a reaction against it in the service book of 1882 but it also stimulated liturgical elaboration to suit the demands of the bourgeoisie in the fashionable chapels. Hymnody flourished at this time, with the *Wesleyan Hymn Book* of 1878 maintaining the layout of the 1780 book but with many new hymns. The *Primitive Methodist Hymnal* marked a new style, with its supplement of 1912 including an interesting mixture of the romantic and the modernistic.

These developments were paralleled elsewhere. *Hymns Ancient and Modern* (1861), a landmark in Anglican worship, was followed by the self-consciously Anglo–Catholic *English Hymnal* (1906), whose musical editor, Ralph Vaughan Williams, set standards for all future hymn books. Wesleyanism produced the *Methodist Hymn Book* of 1904, which enabled Methodists to assimilate the best and some of the worst of Victorian hymnody, but was never as popular as its predecessor or its successors of 1933 and 1983.

## 3. Modern emphases

We have now reached Methodist Union in 1932. Three very different worshipping traditions came together, and their common evangelical Arminian theology made assimilation relatively easy. The first great achievement was the *Methodist Hymn Book* (1933). This book still has over 250 hymns of the original Wesleyan inheritance, the best of the Victorian hymns (including revivalist material) and a fair number of hymns, eclipsing the older styles, from liberal Protestanism of the early twentieth century. It lasted fifty years, a 'record' for modern hymn books.

The second major achievement was the *Book of Offices* (1936) [50]. In some ways it was conservative: Morning Prayer was included for those who needed it, the Communion Service was still virtually the 1662 Prayer Book with the long exhortations and unnecessary verbiage removed, and with the prayer of self-offering following the reception of the bread and wine the basic theology was still evident. The rite of baptism was declaratory, and stress was placed on the vows of the parents (no godparents here!). The wedding and funeral services were somewhat richer than those in the 1928 Prayer Book which, though rejected by Parliament, now came into common use. The Covenant Service had contemporary prayers of adoration, confession and thanksgiving, largely derived from John Hunter and G. B. Robson. These prayers were popular, and their use on other occasions made the service less austere than the older versions. An interesting innovation was an alternative communion rite. This has been called by its detractors a 'liturgical botch' and a patronizing attempt to help non-liturgical devotees to move to a liturgical form, as if the latter were obviously superior. More recently liturgists have realized that it had interesting features – the prayer of oblation precedes the reception of the bread and wine and verses of Charles Wesley's resurrection hymn, 'Love's redeeming work is done' provide a concluding note of Easter joy – and it offered a preferable alternative to the all too-frequent custom of beginning the main rite at the prayer of humble access ('We do not presume to come to thy table . . .') when half the congregation had departed at the end of a preaching service.

---

50. There are abundant advantages in the use of such hallowed forms as these, for they not only unite us with the universal Church of Christ, dispersed throughout all ages and all lands, in one act of worship, but they put into ordered reverent words the most sacred desires and emotions of the Christian soul.

It must not be thought that there is here any attempt to disparage the practice of free prayer, which has always been one of the glories of Methodism . . . But there is no real conflict between free prayer and liturgical prayer, for the most fervent and most helpful prayers that ever came from the inspiration of the moment will be found to owe much in their expression to the remembrance of the language of the Bible, of the great liturgies, and of the hymns of Methodism.

*Source*: Preface to the *Book of Offices*, 1936, probably by Dr Henry Bett.

---

A growing awareness of new congregational needs is illustrated by *Divine Worship* (1935), a useful book of services and prayers. While it reflected the mood of the day, it was rather better than some contemporary forms. For some of those who began to learn the art of conducting worship in the 1940s it fulfilled a useful role, promoting a less effusive style in spontaneous prayer and greater congregational participation. The foundation, also in 1935, of the Methodist Church Music Society, which has made an invaluable contribution over the years, may be seen as another response to congregational needs.

In 1950 the *School Hymn Book of the Methodist*

*Church* appeared, with Rupert Davies as words editor. The book was intended to service the worshipping needs of the Methodist day and boarding schools as well as Sunday schools. It was very much in what can be called the Vaughan Williams, 'English Musical Renaissance' tradition of using a great deal of folksong material but adapting it for modern use. It reflected a proper desire for a higher standard of worship and a firm belief that excellence was attainable. 'The second rate was always out of place because its combination of large returns and small demands (its cheapness!) is out of conformity with the gospel and real life.'[4] Rupert Davies and his co-editors made the assumption that children would actually enjoy singing both the great hymns of the church and the best of the newer ones. That style of pedagogy was soon to prove unfashionable as the existential and the directly contemporary came to be regarded as of overwhelming significance. In the 1950s the book was used by some congregations as its staple hymn book for morning worship on 'all age' occasions, but thereafter it fell out of favour.

During the 1930s, in reaction to liberalism in theology, there was a movement in favour of a greater objectivity in worship, more frequent celebration of the Holy Communion, and greater use of Wesley's hymns. J. E. Rattenbury's book *Vital Elements in Public Worship* (1936) typifies these convictions, which were not limited to members of the Methodist Sacramental Fellowship. Rattenbury had widespread appeal because of his bridging of theological parties. 'If we neglect sacramental worship, we cut ourselves off from the Catholic Church in which we say we believe, but if we neglect evangelism, we cut ourselves off from Methodist history and the Methodist witness.'[5] Alan Kay's *The Nature of Christian Worship* (1953) is in much the same vein. There is no doubt that many post-war ministers were much concerned about worship, seeking a greater richness as well as more contemporary relevance. In the matter of ministerial garb, there was some return to the Reformed dress of gown and bands, with often a cassock replacing the frockcoat and the lounge suit of the 1920s and 1930s. All this ran alongside a strong desire for the congregation to be more actively involved in prayers, in reading the scriptures with a greater attention to biblical theology, then in its heyday, and in preaching. The coincidence of ecumenism, the liturgical movement and biblical theology was crucial in the period before, during and after the war.

## 4. Preaching and popular music

Preaching, still dominant in worship in the 1930s, boasted notable exponents. The older style – doctrinally highly orthodox – was represented by Dr Dinsdale Young, still in full flow at Westminster Central Hall. At one moment, there could be loud laughter, at another tears when a homely story with a moving climax was told. The choir would back up the sermon with appropriate (or not so appropriate!) anthems. The organist, too, knew how to set the mood. No church illustrated the power of preaching better than Brunswick, Leeds. Successively, Alfred E. Whitham, Leslie Weatherhead and William E. Sangster filled the church from 1920 to 1939. Whitham had a delightful mixture of genuine folksiness with deep sacramentalism [51]. Weatherhead, whose *Discipleship* was still a classic in the 1940s, exploited all the discoveries of the new psychology, not only to counsel and help people but in his preaching. He used every device to make Jesus real and contemporary. His theology was liberal Protestant with a deep sense of the historical Jesus, not yet dimmed by the scepticism of the 'form critics'. Weatherhead was not merely a dynamic personality, he had an almost hypnotic skill in blending worship and preaching to make Jesus a living force. From 1936 until his retirement in 1960 he was able to exercise his skill at the City Temple. Sangster was a more conventional evangelical with enormous skill in sermon construction and illustration. He was more 'manly', if that adjective dare be used, and perhaps more in tune with the ordinary men and women of Leeds. Interestingly, during his ministry attendance at Communion increased, though only a tenth of the large congregation were communicants. Sangster's last service at Brunswick in August 1939, before he went to his great ministry at Central Hall, Westminster, was attended by over 2,000 people. When the Second World War began on 3 September, his successor, Garfield Lickes, himself a fine preacher, had a congregation of 200. The 'blackout', in short, began to seal the fate of the Nonconformist tradition of preaching! It is interesting that ninety-eight members of Brunswick joined the forces, eight being killed.

---

51. On my return [from a museum visit] I must have dozed, for I thought I was treading the streets of the Holy City, pottering about like a tourist. In my wandering I came upon the museum of that city of our dreams. I went in, and a courteous attendant conducted me round. There was some old armour there, much bruised with battle. Many things were conspicuous by their absence. I saw nothing of Alexander's nor or Napoleon's. There was no Pope's ring, nor even the inkwell that Luther is said to have thrown at the devil, nor Wesley's seal and keys, nor the first Minutes of Conference, nor the last (I was sorry about that, because my name was in it). I saw a widow's mite and the feather of a little bird. I saw some swaddling clothes, a hammer, and three nails, and a few thorns . . . I saw a sponge that had once been dipped in vinegar, and a small piece of silver . . . Whilst I was turning over a common drinking cup which had a very honourable place, I whispered to the attendant, 'Have you got a towel and basin among your collection?' 'No,' he said, 'not here; you see, they are in constant use.' Then I knew I was in Heaven, in the Holy City, and amid the redeemed society.

*Source*: A. E. Whitham, *The Discipline and Culture of the Spiritual Life*, Hodder & Stoughton 1938, pp. 40–41.

---

Sangster, Soper and Weatherhead formed a remarkable Methodist trio in the 1950s, writing as well as preaching with distinction, but the great preaching tradition ended almost dramatically at the end of that decade. In the 1960s the crowds did not follow the great preachers any more. The reasons are highly complex. The centre of cities became less 'user-friendly,' for example, but there was also a mistrust of authoritarian oratory. Radio or perhaps pedestrian speakers like Baldwin, Chamberlain and Attlee killed it off, replacing it with 'fireside chats' like those of Roosevelt. Again, educationalists tended to write off preaching as an educational medium. They were right, for preaching is not primarily teaching but an attempt to offer a viable faith in a living Lord. The image, moreover, was often overtaking the spoken word as the mode of the message. Be the causes never so complex, rhetoric was even more discredited in the popular mind by Hitler. By the 1960s, the spread of cheap radios and of television enabled people to hear the human voice (as Dr Alan Wilkinson put it) as verbal wallpaper.

The Second World War saw the virtual end of another notable element in Methodist worship. I remember Darlington Street Church, Wolverhampton. My aunt was the chief contralto in a fine choir which sang good quality anthems each week, canticles at each morning service, and oratorios with top soloists three or four times a year. Many a Black Country chapel could put on *The Messiah* or *Elijah* or even *The Dream of Gerontius* – with Isobel Baillie, if they were lucky, to partner my aunt. This was still an enormously creative period of popular music – Huddersfield or Halifax choral societies were stuffed with chapel folk, with Black Dyke Mills or Brighouse and Rastrick bands to give support. A good Yorkshire Methodist congregation like King Cross, Halifax would sing hymns in four-part harmony and the *Te Deum* at the drop of a hat, as well as more popular hymns. Congregational participation could take many forms: exuberant but not raucous singing, for example, could be followed by rapt attention to the preacher. And there were plenty of valued opportunities to hear good preaching, and to assist it. At Darlington Street, Wolverhampton in the 1930s, for example, on the occasion of the Sunday School Anniversary, the local minister would make way for Dr Luke Wiseman from the Home Mission Department; and at King Cross, Halifax, where I was minister from 1981 to 1989, one could still feel the way in which the congregation, by its mood of expectation, caused the preacher to give of his or her best.

## 5. Post-war changes

With the war came great changes. One was a slow evolution of afternoon Sunday School into morning Junior Church. The enormous loss of numbers was not due so much to the change in timing but to underlying sociological pressures. The 'weekend' now took the place of the 'Victorian Sunday' which had lingered on in some areas until the war. Before the war, and in many places until 1960, the largest congregations in town chapels tended to be in the evening. By 1960 the morning congregation had to accommodate a large number of children. Parade Services or Family Worship became obligatory in a church with uniformed organizations or a large Junior Church. But if the preacher could 'pitch' his or her address at the 7–12 age group, there was inevitably a different feel and sometimes difficulties for teenagers. By 1980, except in rare cases, the afternoon Sunday School had gone and, with it, the large numbers of children whose parents did not attend church. Only time will show the real significance of this enormous change.

At another level, the Liturgical Movement in other denominations was having its slow and somewhat late effect on Methodism. In 1945 the Anglican monk Dom Gregory Dix in *The Shape of the Liturgy* (1945) claimed that at the heart of the Lord's supper was a four-fold action – taking, giving thanks, breaking, sharing. We might add the interpretative words about the body and 'the blood of the covenant' as a fifth essential. Liturgical scholars have also shown the significance of early accounts in Justin Martyr (150 CE) and Hippolytus (215 CE) which reveal the probable nature of the service of word and sacrament before the conversion of Constantine. Questions inevitably arose. Was it possible to get behind the stale controversies of the Reformation and Counter-Reformation to a more primitive and irenical form? How could the service, no longer dominated by priest or preacher, become more the people's service? How could a more logical style be found for non-eucharistic worship than the combination of early Wesleyan preaching service and revivalist meeting, with the sermon as the great climax? In Methodism scholars like Raymond George and Gordon Wakefield played a quiet but formative role in the Joint Liturgical Group which wrestled with such issues and produced not only a common two-year lectionary but also forms for a Daily Office and suggestions for Holy Week.

In 1960 Methodism accepted a *Report on Worship* which was positive, though rather conservative. It presented a form of worship clearly in the Reformation tradition – comparison with a similar order in the Church of Scotland's Book of Common Order (1940) shows a line going back to Calvin – and viable as an order when the Holy Communion was not celebrated. The report and parallel experiments in the 1960s acted as catalysts to further action and led to the experimental forms of 1968, which were soon widely used in the Connexion. There was still argument about whether it was appropriate to address God as 'You' but in the Methodist Service Book, finally published in 1975, the 'Thou' form disappeared. This development mirrored what was very common practice, deriving from newer translations of the Bible and from books of prayers such as those of Caryl Micklem.[6] The arrival of a new service book coincided with the clear desire of many people, not just 'high church' ministers, to share in Holy Communion more frequently [52]. Two services of word and sacrament a month (one morning, one evening) became normal in many churches.

---

52. The eucharist is essentially the sacrament of the gift which God makes to us in Christ through the power of the Holy Spirit. Every Christian receives this gift of salvation through communion in the body and blood of Christ. In the eucharistic meal, in the eating and drinking of the bread and wine, Christ grants communion with himself, God himself acts, giving life to the body of Christ and renewing each member. In accordance with Christ's promise, each baptized member of the body of Christ receives in the eucharist the assurance of the forgiveness of sins (Matt. 26.28) and the pledge of eternal life (John 6.51–8). Although the eucharist is essentially one complete act, it will be considered here under the following aspects: thanksgiving to the Father, memorial of Christ, invocation of the Spirit, communion of the faithful, meal of the Kingdom.

*Source: Baptism, Eucharist and Ministry*, WCC, Geneva 1982, p. 10.

The 1960s also saw a clear desire for much more experiment in worship and alternatives to preaching. Wise leaders of worship refused to take an 'either . . . or' stance. Good preaching could exist alongside new styles of drama, the use of slides in the intercessory prayers, films (although the Film Service was a transitory phenomenon) and dialogue. Dialogue, it has to be said, was not always very successful. 'Please, one of you is bad enough, but both is too much,' said a steward, tongue in cheek, at Oxford Place Chapel in 1968! New forms of hymns and songs came into use, paralleling the changes in popular culture from 'skiffle' to the Beatles, and the work of the Anglican Sydney Carter, the most notable of the radical song writers, was represented in *Hymns and Songs* (1969). Methodist writers, typical of the period, are Richard Jones and Geoffrey Ainger. See, for example:

> Born in the night,
>   Mary's child,
> A long way from your home:
>   Coming in need,
>   Mary's child
> Born in a borrowed room.
> (Geoffrey Ainger, 1925–, HS 76/HP 95)

In music the impact of writers like Fr Geoffrey Beaumont (whose style, reminiscent of earlier musical comedy hits, made his work amenable to the older generation) and the Twentieth Century Light Music Group was speedy and pervasive. Following the era of songs of social revolt – 'We Shall Overcome' – came the revival of the religion of the heart and a new stream of 'renewal songs.' In the early 1960s, 'renewal' implied a radical theology and referred to a renewal of social resolve; by the mid-1970s it meant a renewal of revivalism and implied a conservative theology and a charismatic style. The song writer Graham Kendrick has emerged as a writer, some of whose material – 'The Servant King' and 'Meekness and Majesty,' for example – may have survival value.

The compilation of a new hymn book is a perilous proceeding. The Methodist and ecumenical book *Hymns and Psalms* (1983), with Ivor Jones and Richard Jones as music and words editors respec-

tively, made a valiant attempt to combine the old inheritance with a good deal of modern material. The Methodist hymn writer Fred Pratt Green contributed twenty-seven hymns, but Graham Kendrick came too late to be included. Since 1983 many Methodist churches have had the use of supplementary material such as *Songs of Fellowship*, *Mission Praise* and *Power Praise*. Once again the phenomenon we have noticed before has inevitably occurred. Revivalist and popular songs appear alongside traditional hymnody. Each age produces both classical and popular music. If churches and worship-leaders exercise discrimination and common sense, division can be avoided. Much fine music and hymnody come now from sources like Taizé in France or Iona in Scotland. At the same time, even though an authoritative hymn book is a characteristic of Methodism stemming from Wesley's book of 1780 and not lightly to be set aside, the riches of *Hymns and Psalms* have still to be fully explored by many Methodist churches. Take, for example:

> Across the world, across the street,
>   The victims of injustice cry
> For shelter and for bread to eat,
>   And never live until they die.
>
> Then let the servant Church arise,
>   A caring Church that longs to be
> A partner in Christ's sacrifice,
>   And clothed in Christ's humanity.
> (Fred Pratt Green, 1903–, HP 804)

## 6. The Methodist Service Book

A look at the structure of the Sunday Service of 1975 gives a clue to recent liturgical thinking, which is also reflected in developments in the Church of England, the Roman Catholic Church, the United Reformed Church and the Church of Scotland, whose new *Book of Common Order* (1994) is the latest in the series.

Only one order for Holy Communion is given. The structure is threefold: praise and confession, the Word read and preached, the Ministry of the Upper Room. In the first part we have the collect for purity, the commandments of Jesus, the corporate confession, the declaration of forgiveness, the collect of the day and the Gloria. The ministry of the word contains three lessons and the sermon, intercessions follow, several model forms being provided, and are concluded by the Lord's Prayer. Then comes the 'Peace' (which can be as formal or informal as needed), the creed (other recent services place the creed after the sermon), the offering, and the prayer of thanksgiving (which contains all the elements, including congregational acclamations, which liturgical scholars consider appropriate). The opening 'rubrics' or instructions suggest a great deal of congregational participation, with much more variety in styles of prayer than is often realized.

Two or three matters would bewilder Anglican friends visiting a Methodist service. The elements consist of bread, often diced, with a larger piece to break. The wine in the early days of Methodism was fermented but in deference to temperance sentiments it is simply laid down that the 'juice of the grape' should be used. Normally there are individual glasses rather than a chalice. This custom goes back to a germ-conscious generation and clever advertising at the beginning of the century. Increasingly children participate in Holy Communion if they are baptized. Following Communion, the service closes with a brief prayer and a dismissal with the blessing. Hymns and songs are, of course, an integral part of the service.

Other styles of worship need noticing. Methodists believe in and practise 'all-age baptism'. In other words, infants or children who can answer for themselves may appropriately be baptized as well as those for whom baptism is in response to faith. Many churches will have baptisms involving all ages. The service of confirmation includes laying on of hands or the traditional Methodist giving of the 'right hand of fellowship' which marked admission to 'the society'. In Methodism those who have not been confirmed or 'received into full membership' (as the older, now discarded phraseology had it) are placed on a Community Roll. People can be removed from the membership list – a relic of days when Methodism was a society – but are retained on the Community Roll. Confirmation is not repeated if the person returns to regular worship, but the Church Council has to restore the person to membership. In some ways confirmation is still a rite looking for a theology. Some form of commitment is needed in a church which practises the baptism of infants or children.

Services for weddings and funerals are included, with clear instructions about the possibilities of an act of thanksgiving following a civil wedding ceremony. The Methodist theology both of the priesthood of all believers and of the proper role of presbyters or ministers can be noted in the rich services of ordination and commissioning.

Finally, we note that the Communion Service from the Book of Offices of 1936 is included and, of course, the Covenant Service. This book is used widely, though the process of revision is now well under way and experimental services are available. Very wide consultation is being sought by the Faith and Order Committee which is responsible for liturgical material. The 1989 *Report of the Commission on Worship* and the *Commission on Music Making* in 1994 back up the magazine, *Worship and Preaching*, and meanwhile the *Companions to the Lectionary*[7] give pointers to new styles and imaginative innovation.

## 7. Present day worship in Methodism

Let us look at what happens in two average Methodist churches of 150 members.

Once a month Holy Communion will be celebrated in the morning. The minister, in a cassock and bands or a plain suit, will be assisted by readers. Lay people will be involved in the distribution of the bread and wine. The Junior Church will join the congregation for the service of the Upper Room for which they will have received preparation. There will be a blessing for babies and any who prefer not to receive the bread and wine. The order of service will follow the shape of the Sunday Service,[8] the great Prayer of Thanksgiving being used verbatim.

On another Sunday morning the service will be 'All-Age Worship', conducted either by the minister or by a Local Preacher. *Songs of Fellowship* supplements

*Hymns and Psalms*. There will be a great deal of participation. The Junior Church will provide readers and will assist in the prayers. There will be visual material, and there could be drama. The music group may sing. There could well be a baptism, too.

On two other Sunday mornings the service will be a preaching service [53]. One of these will be conducted by a Local Preacher who is a member of the congregation. He or she will use the folkgroup to enrich the service. The Joint Liturgical Group Lectionary (JLG 2, a revised set of readings), though by no means obligatory, will normally be used to provide the scripture readings. The next week the choir will sing festal music as it is Palm Sunday.

---

**53.** *An Outline for a Preaching Service*

Welcome and call to worship
Hymn
Prayer: Invocation and Adoration
Confession. Declaration of Forgiveness
Collect of the Day
Hymn
Old Testament Reading

Psalm (from *Hymns and Psalms* read together)
Reading from the Epistles etc.
Hymn
Reading from the Gospels
Sermon
Hymn
Prayer of Thanksgiving and Intercession
The Lord's Prayer
Notices if not printed. Offering and prayer
Hymn
Blessing and Dismissal

*Sources*: *Sunday Service* 1975 and *Methodist Prayer Handbook* 1995–6.

---

At evening worship, the Holy Communion will be celebrated monthly, using new experimental forms which provide time for silence and meditation.

Once a year the circuit youth will gather for a 'youth service' at which there will be a band, a good deal of modern music, worship songs and, sometimes, a hard hitting sermon! Each year at Christmastide there will be a 'Nativity' service, involving all ages and written by one of the members. A carol service will also be devised. Each year the choir mistress will produce a musical of the Roger Jones variety, again involving all age groups.

Other occasions will be ecumenical: Ash Wednesday, Wednesdays in Lent, Maundy Thursday, Good Friday. Easter Day will include an early service of Holy Communion followed by breakfast, and on Christmas Eve for midnight Communion the church will be lit entirely by candles, with the Lord's Table placed centrally. The Watchnight service will follow a church party, and the Covenant Service will open the New Year on the following Sunday. These particular churches are fortunate to have a team of competent organists and pianists – both organ and piano being used at most services. If children read lessons, they are helped to be audible. Preaching is varied in style – a twenty-minute exposition on occasions, a liturgical sermon at Holy Communion, a free ranging participatory style at All-Age Worship, and a short 'Thought for the Day' at early morning communion.

This is a snapshot of just two ordinary churches – one in Yorkshire, one in Lancashire. Others may be more traditional – a service with a sermon as the conclusion is still very common. Others may be more adventurous or more 'charismatic'. Non-Methodists will note the role of Local Preachers who are trained in the practicalities of worship, in preaching, biblical studies and theology.[9] On the second Sunday in May in 1995 out of the 410 services of worship in the 305 Methodist Churches in Cornwall, 247 were led by Local Preachers, compared with 113 by ministers, and 50 were covered by other arrangements. In some churches Local Preachers form a 'team' with a minister and will share in the Holy Communion. The smaller churches are enabled to have regular worship through people like the six Local Preachers at our typical medium-sized chapel. The team of organists there helps two village chapels, one of them now a prayer and conference centre to which groups can go and enjoy a meal, worship, fellowship and a walk on the moors. One of the villages is rapidly becoming a small commuter suburb with consequent church growth.

Our exploration has taken us from the 'Foundery', John Wesley's first London headquarters in 1739, to Lancashire and Yorkshire in the late 1990s. There are common characteristics right through the 250 years, not least a proper desire that Christ shall be offered to the people.

## For discussion

1. What do you think of Charles Wesley's hymns? Are they as marvellous as Bernard Manning and others thought? Are there other hymns more suitable for us?

2. Do you prefer prayer to be responsive or entirely spontaneous or both? Why? What are the strengths and weaknesses of either?

3. Evaluate the Covenant Service. Why is it poorly attended?

4. What sort of sermon do you prefer? What is the purpose of preaching?

5. 'Mum, I'm bored.' What can we do to avoid that cry from teenagers? Or have teenagers always said it?

6. What changes would you like in the new service book?

7. Argue for and against 'All-Age Worship'. Why do some teenagers dislike it?

8. Why do you think that in Christian history more women than men have attended worship regularly?

# 7

# Methodism and the Wider Church

In 1942, at the height of the Second World War when victory over Nazism seemed a precarious hope, William Temple wrote [54]:

> 54. As though in preparation for such a time as this, God has been building up a Christian fellowship which now extends into almost every nation, and binds citizens of them all together in true unity and mutual love. No human agency has planned this. It is the result of the great missionary enterprise of the last hundred and fifty years . . . Almost incidentally the great world fellowship has arisen, it is the great new fact of our era . . .
>
> *Source*: W. Temple, *The Church Looks Forward*, Macmillan 1944, p. 2.

Many see the World Missionary Conference at Edinburgh in 1910, in which Methodists like the American layman, J. R. Mott, played a crucial role, as the beginning of the ecumenical movement. Mott's vision of 'the evangelization of the world in our generation' is a measure of the enormous Christian idealism at the turn of the century. As a result of the changing climate, the English Free Churches began to see the possibility of federation through the National Council of Evangelical Free Churches, elected on a representative basis and set up in 1896. Later, in 1919, the Federal Council of the Evangelical Free Churches was inaugurated, the somewhat lukewarm Wesleyans joining a year later. As early as 1908, however, John

Scott Lidgett, in his Presidential address to the Wesleyan Methodist Conference, had stressed the primary importance of the 'unifying of Christendom' [55].

> 55. Where there are no differences, our watchword must be union; where they are comparatively slight, federation; where they are more serious yet not destructive of the fundamental agreement with Christianity, co-operation in order to defend and promote the supreme interests and applications of our common Christian life.
>
> *Source*: J. S. Lidgett, *Apostolic Ministry*, Culley 1909, pp. 15–16.

Thereafter, these Free Church bodies ran on parallel and somewhat confusing lines until their amalgamation in 1940. There is now strong Methodist representation on the Free Church Federal Council, and the Revd Dr Kathleen Richardson succeeded the Revd Dr John Newton as Moderator. It must be admitted that the Council has done little to bring about full federation, let alone union, between the Free Churches. Much of its work was taken up by the British Council of Churches and, more recently, by Churches Together. Not until 1972, with the establishment of the United Reformed Church, did the most obvious union (seen as desirable by Bernard Manning in 1933) become a fact. It comprised the Presbyterian Church of England with its large Scottish influence, a majority of the Congregational Church (formerly Union), and later some of the Churches of Christ.

Nevertheless the Free Church Council provided a valuable clearing house for negotiations which followed the important and irenic *Appeal to All Christian Peoples* from the Lambeth Conference of 1920.[1] The debate of the 1920s, in fact, laid down the lines of future ecumenical approaches, not least to the protracted but eventually successful negotiations in South India. To these Methodism made a very important contribution when, in 1934, the Conference approved the prototype of the South India scheme with its mutual acceptance of ministries and consequent episcopal system. This decision was largely influenced by the outstanding advocacy of W. F. Lofthouse, Principal of Handsworth College, Birmingham. Future conflicts were foreshadowed, however, in that Lofthouse's colleague, the historian Henry Bett, pointed out the dangers of episcopacy, taking the position held by Bernard Manning that, as at the Reformation, there can be continuity of faith when continuity of ministerial succession is broken.

In the 1930s the Friends of Reunion, aided by the Student Christian Movement, brought church leaders together, and in 1936 there appeared *A Sketch of a United Church*. W. F. Lofthouse, though a strong supporter of the South India scheme, which also involved an acceptance of episcopacy, was less happy with these proposals. The Sketch was followed by an *Outline of a Reunion Scheme for the Church of England and the Free Churches of England* (1938) to which the Free Churches made a final, somewhat negative reply in 1941. That particular matter stood still until Archbishop Geoffrey Fisher's sermon about Intercommunion in November 1946. Fisher, in a famous phrase, invited the Free Churches to 'take episcopacy into their system'.

There were also ecumenical ventures on a world scale, culminating in the establishment of the World Council of Churches in 1948. Two bodies, Faith and Order and Life and Work, both of which had already held important international conferences, came together at this point, and were joined in 1961 by the International Missionary Council. The IMC's conference at Jerusalem in 1928 was especially significant, revealing openness to other faiths and to the contribution of the younger churches. When the next conference was held at Tambaram in 1938, however, the theological climate had changed and the influence of Karl Barth, who drew a sharp distinction between religion and Christian faith, was apparent in Hendrik Kraemer's preparatory volume. The 1924 conference on Christian Politics, Economics and Citizenship, which aimed to establish a 'norm for Christian thought and action for the further working out of Christian order', foreshadowed a good deal of the thinking which lay behind the creation of the 'Welfare State' of the post-1945 era. There was notable input from Methodists like W. R. Maltby, Henry Carter, Benson Perkins, Ryder Smith, S. E. Keeble, the young Donald Soper and the formidable figure of W. F. Lofthouse who, with his trenchantly Protestant and yet deeply sympathetic approach to the breadth of Christian tradition, appears as a weighty Methodist spokesman at most of the pre-war ecumenical conferences. His statement of Methodist theology at the Lausanne Conference was particularly noteworthy. The later conferences on Life and Work at Oxford in 1937 and in the same year at Edinburgh on Faith and Order were overshadowed by the menace of Hitler.

A new Methodist voice emerged at this time in R. Newton Flew of Wesley House, Cambridge. Flew's influence is apparent in the important Methodist statement on *The Nature of the Christian Church According to the Teaching of the Methodists* (1937), which has only been superseded by a new statement, *Called to Love and Praise*, in 1995. The 1937 statement was backed up by Flew's *Jesus and His Church* (1938), which parallels in some ways the more famous book by the young Michael Ramsey, *The Gospel and the Catholic Church* (1936). Both represented new emphases deriving from biblical theology and amounting almost to a rediscovery of the doctrine of the church.

The church of the New Testament, Flew stressed, is not to be understood as a certain number of individuals who have formed themselves into an association for a common purpose. It is not a club or a religious society of a type familiar in the Graeco–Roman world. As the body of Christ, the church is formed by those who are in communion with God, owes its very existence to God's revelation of himself and is pledged to be God's instrument for his age-long purpose.

---

**56.** The message of the Church is the gospel or Word of God. It is the function of the Church to understand, interpret and proclaim this Word . . . the Church of Christ proclaims Christ even more by what it is than by what it says . . . Both sacraments are . . . modes of proclaiming the Word which is Christ himself, active in the life of the church . . . it is clear that we cannot speak of 'the threefold ministry' as claiming the authority of the New Testament. Further, there is no evidence that definite prerogatives or powers are to be transmitted . . . the true continuity with the Church of past ages which we cherish is to be found in the continuity of the Christian experience, the fellowship in the gift of the one Spirit; in the continuity of the allegiance to one Lord, the continued proclamation of the message, the continued acceptance of the mission . . . The bread of life is the gift of God, but it is broken from hand to hand . . . Behind each believer of to-day there stretches a long chain, each link a Christian man or woman, till we find ourselves, with the first disciples, in the company of the Lord himself . . . This is our doctrine of apostolic succession.

*Source*: *The Nature of the Christian Church according to the Teaching of the Methodists*, Methodist Publishing House 1937, pp. 17, 18, 19, 24, 30.

---

Not all these points, to Flew's chagrin, were made clear in later negotiations but he chaired the WCC Faith and Order Commission when, at the Conference in Lund in 1952, the principle that churches should not do separately what they could do together was laid down. When *The Nature of the Church* volume was prepared for Lund, Flew not only included a shortened version of the Methodist statement quoted here [56], but also, with total impartiality, wrote the sections on the Church of Rome. At that Conference, it should be noted, the Scottish theologian Thomas Torrance swung the commission away from comparing what each confession said about itself (comparative ecclesi-ology) to looking at what they said about Christ himself (comparative christology).

In later Faith and Order matters Rupert Davies replaced Flew as a leading Methodist representative. More recently, Professor Geoffrey Wainwright has done fine, irenic work at The Queen's College, Birmingham, Union Theological Seminary, New York, and Duke University. He chaired the Lima Conference which produced the key document *Baptism, Eucharist and Ministry* in 1982. We can spotlight, too, the contributions of Dr D. T. Niles, Dr Pauline Webb, and Dr Philip Potter, a West Indian, who was General Secretary, 1972–1984, and Emilio Castro from Uruguay from 1985 to 1992, as the WCC, rightly, reflected the concerns of the African, Asian and South American churches as well as those from North America and Europe. Methodists continued to play their part, though never perhaps so notably as in the early Assemblies, such as Amsterdam (1948), Evanston (1954) and New Delhi (1961) from which the call came for 'one church renewed for mission'.

But we must return to Great Britain. Local Councils of Churches in places like Bristol and Bolton had been in existence for some years, but in 1942 the British Council of Churches (BCC) came into existence. Methodism has always played a lively part, and Harry O. Morton (1925–1988) was the very able General Secretary from 1973 to 1980. The Council, like the WCC, did not include Roman Catholics, though Catholics are involved in the new structures which replaced the BCC in 1990. The BCC has often enough made use of Methodist expertise, and Henry Carter, Edward Rogers, Brian Duckworth and Kenneth Greet have been especially prominent when issues of social responsibility have been discussed. In 1964 the BCC, boldly taking up the theme of the WCC New Delhi Conference of 1961, affirmed the possibility of church union on the South India model (1947) being achieved in Britain by 1980. Such idealism, tempered by the church leaders who met in 1972, proved to be over-optimistic. Nevertheless, other matters handled by the BCC, like arrangements for the common use of church buildings and the widespread establishment of what are now called Local Ecumenical Partnerships (the new town of Milton Keynes is an outstanding example), were of great significance. Methodism has been in the forefront here. Many of our churches are linked with the United Reformed Church, some with Baptists, and quite a few with the Church of England. Through their pastoral involvement in such situations, many ministers of other communions are 'recognized and regarded' as equivalent to Methodist ministers. The federalism envisaged by some of the early ecumenical pioneers has come about not through large schemes but through local initiative and enterprise.

We return to Archbishop Fisher's initiative in 1946 and the increasing cordiality among the churches which it sparked off. Geoffrey Fisher suggested that, to secure full communion with the Church of England, the Free Churches should accept a church order involving bishops, 'thus securing a ministry mutually acceptable to all'. Behind this proposal is undoubtedly the so-called Lambeth Quadrilateral, which affirmed Holy Scripture, the Creeds, the sacraments of Baptism and Holy Communion, and the episcopate 'locally adopted'. Fisher's initiative led to multi-church discussions and the report *Church Relations in England* (1950), which stressed that existing divisions were 'within the Body of Christ' and offered a clear statement of underlying theological agreement between the mainstream communions. The crux was the doctrine of the ministry: Anglican insistence on episcopal ordination, Free Church refusal of any form of reordination of their ministers. The Report was commended to the Free Churches. The Baptist Union did not feel able to take up the matter, maintaining that the time was not ripe for union discussions. The Presbyterians and Congregationalists were beginning the long haul to their union in 1972. Methodism gave a positive reply, wishing negotiations to begin with three provisos:

1. that the Church of England acknowledges that our divisions are within the Christian Body which is throughout in a state of schism. (That all parties should recognize each other as within the body of Christ, despite their divisions, was clearly crucial.)

2. that the same liberty of interpretation of the nature of episcopacy and of priesthood would be accorded to the Methodist Church as prevails in the Church of England. (Yes, said the Anglicans, 'so long as the office of priest in the Church of God is safeguarded'. Much confusion might have been avoided if some attempt had been made to define 'priesthood' at this point.)

3. that the Methodist Church would be free to preserve the relations of intercommunion and fellowship with non-episcopal churches which it now enjoys. (This matter had to be repeatedly made clear.)

In 1955 representatives were appointed by both churches. The Methodist team was led by the resourceful Dr Harold Roberts, Principal of Richmond College. The first report of the Anglican–Methodist Unity Commission in 1958 sparked off the great debate which continued until 1972. It was clear that they had gone far beyond Dr Fisher's limited goal. Their aim is nothing less than the visible unity of the whole Church of Christ. This is asserted clearly at all stages [57].

---

57. The aim set before us is not the forging of an attractive and imposing ecclesiastical organization, but a new obedience to the manifest will of God. We are being called with ever greater urgency to further the mission of the Church, overseas as well as at home, by the deepening of our unity to serve our nation as one servant Church, to teach the people of our nation with one Christian doctrine, and with one voice to present to the world our crucified and risen Saviour.

*Source: Towards Reconciliation: The Interim Statement of the Anglican Methodist Unity Commission*, SPCK and Epworth Press, 1967, p. 5.

---

In 1958 common ground is asserted – who God is, the person and work of Christ, the scriptures as the supreme rule of faith and practice, the Apostles' and Nicene Creeds summing up the heart of the faith, the sacraments as of divine institution and perpetual obligation, a ministry set apart for a life-long task. This somewhat slick statement had to be elaborated and it had honestly to be made clear that there are varied ways of looking at scripture held in both churches and that doctrinal divisions go across the denominations from conservative evangelicals to radicals. The same is true of priesthood and ministry. Christ alone is priest in his own right. The church corporately is a 'royal priesthood' with each believer having his or her own ministry of worship and witness, service and sacrifice. Some Anglicans hold that episcopal ordination confers, beside grace and authority, an indelible priestly character and that episcopally ordained ministers alone may preside at Holy Communion and pronounce absolution. Other Anglicans value episcopacy highly but deny that any part of the minister's task is priestly in any sense beyond that in which the whole church's worship is priestly. Differences in Methodism are also acknowledged, though not in terms of structured parties.

Full liberty of interpretation is demanded. Each church has its special 'gifts', and the Anglicans lay great stress on the 'episcopate as it emerged in the clear light of history from the time when definite evidence begins to be available'. It is possible, even so, for Methodists and Anglicans to search together for what 'episcopacy can become for us and our children'. Methodists state some of their distinctive emphases – the stress on faith, assurance and Christian perfection, Wesley's hymns and a connexional system. It is all very characteristic of the 1940s and 1950s without a whiff of the theological storms to break in the 1960s.

Then comes the 'Scheme' which runs through all the reports (1958, 1963, 1967, 1968). Here is its final form. Stage One we will call the 'engagement'. Inter-communion between two parallel churches is proposed, and a universally acceptable ministry is to be secured through a 'service of reconciliation' with mutual laying-on of hands. Methodism would accept bishops, and episcopal ordination would be the norm for the future. A common ordination service is provided which uses the word 'presbyter' for ministers or priests. This is the scriptural term *presbyteros* with none of the offensive overtones (to the Protestant) of the word 'priest', meaning an ecclesiastic thrust between a believer and his or her maker.

The crux is the 'service of reconciliation'. The intention is to bring unity by an act of commitment in a public liturgical action. There is no denial of any gifts and graces already given but rather an 'openness to the future' in which God will give any further grace or commission or authority needed. Right at the beginning of the action each participating minister affirms that he (no women ministers in either church yet) has been ordained to the ministry of word and sacrament. There follows a reception of representative laity and the ministry by the laying-on of hands. The aim is a ministry fully acceptable in each church. The intention of the rites is an act of mutual recommissioning. It is frankly feared that some Anglicans will see the rite as tantamount to the ordination for the first time of the Methodist ministry. Deliberate ambiguity is admitted, though subterfuge or dishonesty is denied. Any Anglicans who wish to believe that Methodist ministers are being ordained in this service will know that Methodists and many Anglicans will deny this. All in each church who think that ordination is not involved will have to accept in advance that some Anglicans participating believe otherwise. Other alternatives are shown to be even more problematic. Thirty years afterwards the rationale seems incredibly ambiguous but for many it seemed the only way through to full inter-communion.

Stage Two we will call the 'marriage'. What problems do couples face? Where will they live? What house will they live in? How will they relate to their neighbours? No blueprint was laid down. It would take a generation to work out not a 'merger' or a 'take over bid' but a 'real union'. The revolutionary implications for an established church were not fully realized at the time.

Opposition to 'the scheme' built up in the 1960s and preoccupied many. Some Anglo–Catholics felt that 'the service of reconciliation' was ambiguous about priesthood. The former Archbishop Fisher consistently considered it dishonest. Evangelicals saw it as unnecessary. The forming of the 'old alliance' of extremes which has hindered change before in the

Church of England finally produced a sizeable minority of opposition which 'ditched' the scheme.

In 1963, Methodist dissentients – Professor Kingsley Barrett, Dr Norman Snaith, Revd Thomas Meadley and Professor Thomas Jessop – stated that episcopacy, not being laid down in scripture, should not be required. Rather, there should be a recognition of ministers as they are. They went on to express anxiety about the likely absorption of Methodism into Anglicanism and about the service of reconciliation being interpreted as ordination. Moreover, they found it difficult to square the use of 'priest' in the report with the view of ministry in the Methodist Deed of Union and were convinced that Methodism's participation in the new united church at Stage Two would make it 'very improbable that it will be in communion with non-episcopal churches'. Again, they asked whether there would be a 'closed' communion table and stricter marriage disciplines, and they predicted that splits would occur in both churches. Unity, they were convinced, is of the Spirit and not of the structure.

In radical circles, too, there was discontent: Colin Morris, for example, said that the whole business of ecclesiastical joinery was 'like a bald man selling hair restorer', and he asked how relevant it was to the urgent questions of the day, epitomized by the man found dead outside his house in Zambia with nothing but a ball of grass in his belly.

---

58. The advantages of union would be:

1. It would get rid of the irrelevance of present division.
2. It would end wasteful competition.
3. It would mean the sharing of educational facilities.
4. Ministers and laity could be trained together.
5. Common policies could be pursued in the educational sphere.
6. Evangelism and church planting could be facilitated in new areas.

Sources: J. M. Turner, Conflict and Reconciliation, Epworth Press 1985, pp. 202 (adapted); Conversations between the Church of England and the Methodist Church, SPCK and Epworth Press 1963, pp. 51–52.

---

There was, in all this, an undervaluing of what have been called 'non-theological factors' [58]. Wide social mobility and changing cultural patterns have now broken down the denominational and class distinctions which often lurk behind them. Some remain – Methodists, for example, dislike establishment with its hidden power and pomp and its assumption of effortless superiority. At the time of the Conversations, certainly, many Methodists thought the Church of England's worship dull, its laity deprived of influence and its clergy immovable. They were puzzled, moreover, by what seemed its laxity on some personal moral issues (e.g. drink and gambling) and its severity on others (e.g. marriage of divorced persons). Anglicans, by and large, did not know the Methodists very well but disliked what they saw as a corporate inferiority complex. They were annoyed by the apparently idolatrous respect shown to John Wesley, and puzzled by the fact that Methodist ministers seemed always on the move. What they saw as laxity on moral issues, like the re-marriage of divorced people, and harshness on other matters, like the use of alcohol, produced the reverse of Methodist dislikes. In many cases people in both churches whose loyalties were local stressed these objections with dogged perseverance and revealed styles of thinking already a generation or two out of date. Dr David Clark's Between Pulpit and Pew (1982) on the church in Staithes in the North East shows the extremes to which these attitudes can be taken. Middle-of-the-road people in both churches could combine easily, those on the edges could not.

Notwithstanding widespread dissent, fostered by bodies like The Voice of Methodism and including a hearing in the Court of Chancery in 1970, the Methodist Church endorsed 'The Scheme' by majorities ranging from over 50% in Circuit Quarterly meetings, to 77.4% at Conference in July 1969 and 79.4% in 1970, i.e. above the 75% required in both churches. The opposition, which included Methodist intellectuals of the stature of Sir Herbert Butterfield, who feared the blunting of the edge of what he called 'insurgent Christianity', was far from negligible. But Methodism remained true to its statement

59. So long as Christians of one communion part company with Christians of another communion at the Table of the Lord, it is improbable that the world will believe that they hold the secret of a fellowship which overlaps religious, cultural, economic and racial differences. The quest of Christian unity assumes an urgency which cannot be exaggerated, when the disabling consequences of our divisions are seen against the background for a generation which so often either repudiates Christian values or dissociates them from the Christian faith (1952).

Conference affirms its belief that the Will of Christ is that churches should be organically united for mission (1972).

*Source*: The Methodist Conference, *Minutes*, 1952, 1972.

61. It is not the first time that Methodists have been the leaders of Christianity in this country . . . In these latter years we Anglicans have liked to think of ourselves as being the leaders in the matter of Christian unity. But at the moment we are not – the Methodists (and he banged the table with his fist) – it is the Methodists who are the leaders now.

*Source*: O. Chadwick, *Michael Ramsey. A Life*, OUP 1991, p. 341.

of 1952, reiterated at Conference in 1972 [59]. The Church of England was unable to secure the needed majority, despite passionate support of the scheme from Archbishop Michael Ramsey, himself very much on the Catholic side of Anglicanism. The final voting on 3 May 1972 in the General Synod is shown below [60]. It may be that the scheme had not been taken seriously enough in the Church of England, which somehow escaped the agonies which Methodism went through. The tradition of corporate separation prevailed over the concept of 'one church renewed for mission'. Archbishop Michael Ramsey's disappointment at the failure of the scheme was obvious [61].

Disappointment was great in some Methodist circles, especially in the higher echelons of leadership typified by the former Secretary of Conference, Dr Eric Baker. Never again could Anglo–Catholics expect such charity to their views. This was the death blow to the 'mutual reconciliation' style which, ironically, was accepted in North India and Pakistan in 1970.

The radical backlash expected by some did not occur. In Methodism, as elsewhere, life had to go on. The number of candidates for presbyteral ministry began to increase, and women were soon ordained. There was renewed interest in the theology of experience and, with some, a renewed concern for evangelism. The Home Mission Department endorsed the World Methodist Council's call to evangelism – parallel Anglican initiatives in the 1970s stemmed from Archbishop Coggan – and produced much positive material. Others, for whom world population, world poverty, pollution, racism, and the continued threat of thermo-nuclear war were the big issues, emphasized what Edward Rogers called 'a Nonconformity against all that degrades people'. Ecumenism came to be expressed locally: by 1970 there were 325 local projects, and The Sharing of Church Buildings Act (1969) and Canon B15A, allowing limited intercommunion in Anglican churches, were positive and practical steps.

The United Reformed Church, established in 1972, joined with Methodism to produce new initiatives and the Churches Unity Commission published the *Ten Propositions* in January 1976. The Commission reaffirmed the belief that 'the visible unity in life and mission of Christ's people is the Will of God'. The idea

60.

| | | |
|---|---|---|
| Bishops: 34 for, 6 against. | 85% in favour. | |
| Clergy: 152 for, 80 against | 65.62% in favour. | |
| Laity: 147 for, 87 against. | 62.82% in favour. | |

*Source*: A. M. G. Stephenson, *Anglicanism at the Lambeth Conferences*, SPCK 1978, p. 265.

of a 'Covenant' was brought back into the debate, a matter spurred on by the fact that in 1975 the Church in Wales, the Presbyterian Church in Wales, the Methodist Church and the United Reformed Church entered into a Covenant towards Union in Wales. To some this seemed a very limited move, but it has proved more realistic than the English approaches to ecumenism. The Ten Propositions proposed mutual recognition as a beginning but the crucial Proposition 6 pointed to a renewed ministry [62].

---

**62.** We agree to recognize as from an accepted date the ordained ministries of the other Covenanting Churches as true ministries of the Word and Sacrament in the Holy Catholic Church and we agree that all subsequent ordinations to the ministries of the Covenanting Churches shall be according to a common ordinal which will properly incorporate the episcopal, presbyteral and lay roles in ordination.

*Source*: Churches' Unity Commission *Visible Unity. The Ten Propositions*, 1976, p. 2.

---

Methodists involved at this stage included Kenneth Greet, Alan Davies, John Richardson, Dr Stephen Travis and Dr Geoffrey Wainwright. The Methodists, the URCs, the Moravians and the Churches of Christ joined a somewhat muted Anglican response, while the Roman Catholics, the Baptists and the Congregational Federation withdrew. The Churches' Council for Covenanting, chaired by Bishop Kenneth Woollcombe with the Methodist lawyer, Philip Capper, as Secretary, included Kenneth Greet, Geoffrey Wainwright, John Job, Christina Le Moignan, John Stacey, David Tripp and Ernest R. Taylor. The Covenant was produced in 1980. Decisions were to be taken in 1982, which proved to be fatally hasty, thus confirming Archbishop Robert Runcie's grave misgivings.

The somewhat complex proposals had as their object a far greater sharing of Christian resources than had hitherto been possible. A 'National Service of Reconciliation' avoided any hint of re-ordination, though future ordinations would be episcopal. The style of episcopacy in Methodism was to be a matter for internal decision. In the event Adrian Hastings has called it 'a too hastily constructed expression of a form of ecumenical idealism almost at the end of its wits to find a way forward'. This may be harsh, but a memorandum of dissent by Anglican members of the Commission, including Bishop Leonard (now a Roman Catholic), on matters like women ministers and non-episcopal Moderators in the URC, pointed to Anglican inability to find the required majority. The scheme was endorsed by the other churches, despite convinced opposition from Methodists of the calibre of Professor Kingsley Barrett, who could not stomach any form of the historic episcopate.

Dr Kenneth Greet expressed the disappointment of many [63]. The Bishop of Durham, Dr John Habgood, made the same point in *The Times* on 13 July 1982. Of the Free Churches he said: 'After making a huge leap in committing themselves to accept episcopacy, they now find themselves rejected on grounds they can only regard as unreasonable. The Church of England would be foolish to expect a similar opportunity to recur.'

---

**63.** The way marked out by a whole generation of ecumenical leaders has proved to be a cul-de-sac. We must pray that a new generation will succeed where we have failed, for in the end a way must be found. The Holy Spirit does not declare a moratorium just because we temporarily lose our way.

*Source*: A. Hastings, *Robert Runcie*, Mowbray 1991, p. 129.

---

The route to organic union had been blocked. In Scotland, where no episcopacy was involved, the Methodist Synod rejected union with the Church of Scotland. In Wales, the Covenant idea was proving fruitful. In England, ecumenism had to take new or more local forms. The sociologist Bryan Wilson, who had expressed cynicism about what he called 'ecumenicalism' as a clerical obsession in the 1960s, points to the charismatic movement [64].

**64.** The movement reflected the secular concerns of the period of its emergence with the demands, for example, among beatniks, hippies, encounter groups, and others for spontaneity, immediacy, personal freedom of expression and the elevation of experience above intellect . . . charismatic renewal probably did more in a few years to promote a certain type of ecumenical practice than had been achieved in decades by the formal proceedings of church assemblies and committees.

*Source*: B. Wilson, art. 'New Images of Christian Community' in J. S. McManners (ed), *The Oxford Illustrated History of Christianity*, OUP 1990, p. 587.

Wilson makes an important point. The balance of churchmanship in the mainstream churches was shifting, but new styles were not confined to charismatics. The Church of Rome increasingly entered the scene. Both the Church of England and the Methodist Church were engaged in theological conversations which proceeded steadily, even if papal conservatism in Rome itself was not helpful. Union among non-Roman churches is no longer a priority. The 'local' has become more significant. Full intercommunion, equally, is no longer a primary goal. The slogan 'one church renewed for mission' has been replaced by 'diversity of mission' – a change not unrelated to a shift in study of the New Testament from stressing its unity to focussing on its diversity.

It is still far too early to evaluate the Inter-Church Process, popularly called 'Not Strangers but Pilgrims', which underlay the highly significant Swanwick Conference of September 1987. Cardinal Basil Hume played a key role, as did Archbishop John Habgood, in pioneering a mechanism of ecumenical co-operation which replaced the British Council of Churches. The Church of Rome plays a full part in the new structures. There is an overseeing Council of Churches for Britain and Ireland (CCBI) and Churches Together in England (CTE), Action of Churches Together in Scotland (ACTS) and Churches Together in Wales (CTW). Regional and local organizations mediate between the national and local with especial concern for local ecumenical partnerships. It is ironic that before Meth-

odist union both Wesleyan and Primitive Methodist leaders like Scott Lidgett and A. S. Peake saw the goal as organic union, while Free Church theologians like P. T. Forsyth were more immediately concerned with Federation – 'the united states of the church', he called it. We call it 'conciliar fellowship' now. A new process, *Called to be One*,[2] reveals what could be exciting styles of new initiatives in the next decade. There are now some two thousand 'Local Churches Together' or local ecumenical partnerships in England alone. Local ecumenical projects are increasing, many of them single congregations embracing varied traditions. For instance St George's Church, Westhoughton, has Anglican, Methodist and United Reformed constituents and new Christians meeting in a now Anglican day school with varied forms of worship including the eucharist. The Church of Christ in Darnall, Sheffield, is another, uniting three congregations including Methodists. Co-operation in Merseyside or Milton Keynes now typifies what can be done at an intermediate level between the churches, including Roman Catholics. A whole series of tentative new talks are now opening up in England, Wales and Scotland which could pull institutional ecumenism out of the doldrums, though the Called to be One process is realistic about the possibilities. Methodists may be a little chary at anything less than total recognition of ordained ministries with the possibility of new styles of episcopacy avoiding the older styles of hierarchy.

One last matter must not be forgotten. British Methodism is part of a world-wide family of churches which owe their origins to the Wesleyan revival. The World Methodist Council effectively began at a Conference in London in 1881 which was followed by ecumenical conferences embracing World Methodism, firstly once a decade and then twice a decade. While the Council, organized in its present form in 1951, has no executive power over its member churches, it facilitates mission and evangelism, exchanging of pastorates, and the very fruitful Oxford Theological Institute with a conference every five years. Increasingly this hears the voices of Methodists from Africa, Asia and South America. The Council has engaged in dialogue with the Roman Catholic Church,

Lutherans, the Reformed, Orthodox and Anglicans. The World Federation of Methodist Women has meetings prior to the Conference of the WMC. A World Methodist Peace Award has been granted to eminent peace makers such as Sadie Paterson (Northern Ireland), the late President Sadat of Egypt and Lord Soper. In recent years Dr Donald English has been an outstanding chairperson of the World Methodist Council which represents a world community of about fifty million people. Indeed Methodism does still look upon the whole world as its parish.

## For discussion

1. Do you find the Ecumenical Movement something vital to your Christian commitment?

2. Is it really contrary to the New Testament to have different churches, or is diversity a good thing?

3. Are divisions within the churches rather than across denominational boundaries?

4. Why do you think the conversations between the Church of England and Methodism failed and the Covenant proposals too?

5. What do the new 'Churches Together' structures means in your area and to your church?

6. Have we put too much stress on the church as vital part of Christian faith?

7. What should be, do you think, the next stage in relationship between the churches?

# 8

# Methodism – Youth and Age

There is a cricket incident told by Neville Cardus, part of which he invented in order to unearth an inner meaning. Dick Tyldesley, the hugely rotund Lancashire off-spinner of the 1920s, appeared to take a catch low down in the gully. As the batsman began to walk, Tyldesley indicated that the ball had touched the ground before he got his fingers on it. At the close of play Cardus complimented him on his sportsmanship. Tyldesley replied 'Westhoughton Sunday School, tha knows'. Westhoughton Sunday School in Bolton still flourishes, though it is called 'Sunday Club' now! In the country as a whole, however, this century has seen a catastrophic decline of this particular Christian enterprise which gave millions of youngsters a 'folk religion' which, with all its faults, was basically Christian. Today, by contrast, we are part of a post-Christian society with only the after-music of a former faith to be heard. Yet I would hazard the opinion that some of the most successful and interesting work done by the Methodist Church this century has been among young people, despite the following ominous statistics. In 1900 there were nearly two million children in Methodist Sunday Schools; in 1950 there were still a million young people on Methodist premises each week; in 1995 the figure was around 300,000, indicating that most children now associated with churches are there because of parental involvement.

## 1. Sunday Schools

We look, first, at the Sunday School as a product of the second wave of the Evangelical Revival. To see it as a mechanism of bourgeois social control is much too glib. It was much more a means of self-improvement, dominated in West Yorkshire and Lancashire by 'labour aristocrats' rather than millowners, though Mackintosh, the toffee king of Halifax, loved his Sunday School work. Clearly, the Victorian Sunday School gave a veneer of Protestant religion to millions of working-class children. It is easy to caricature 'treats', 'bunfights', and children in white dresses on a platform at the 'sermons' (as the 'Anniversary' is still known in Lancashire!). We should remember, however, that the 'feasts' of Victorian Nonconformity countered what were thought less wholesome community activities. Sunday Schools provided not only much impetus to the elementary education which working-class parents wanted for their children but also the 'invisible religion' which Richard Hoggart, reflecting on his Leeds boyhood, depicts so well in *The Uses of Literacy* (1958).

Sunday Schools, moreover, being often on a different 'trust' from the chapel, could be free of hierarchies and parsons and thus more widely influential. If 'class meetings' reached their thousands, Sunday Schools reached their millions. Here was a bridge between folk-culture and domestic religiosity, whose debacle has not been fully analysed. Some sociologists, however, are now beginning to suggest that the Sunday School contributed greatly to that strange stability of inter-war Britain and that its decline contributed to the subsequent destabilization.

At Methodist Union in 1932 there were 1,300,000 children in Sunday Schools. This was the hey-day at the Graded Sunday School, the brainchild of George Hamilton Archibald of Westhill College and E. H. Hayes. Archibald's idea, influenced by Froebel and other educational psychologists, was to separate children according to age and aptitude. Teaching was to be tempered – and here we see the beginnings of the pervasive influence of Piaget's work on child development – to the age of the child. This strategy linked with the concept so dominant in secular education. Children could be children. 'The Child in the Midst' was the name of the game, though the Bible was still a dominant factor and children could have a grasp of the 'story' with its heroes and villains. Rupert Davies, chaplain at Kingswood School, Bath, summed up the aims of a Sunday School in 1951 [65].

His was an almost frightening agenda. In 1939 a Conference report suggested that all was not well, and the absence of many young men during the war did not help matters. Around 1960, when there had been some stability in membership of the church, a clutch of important reports from the Free Church Council and the British Council of Churches revealed a major crisis in Christian education at all levels. A Methodist report, *The Way Ahead*, appeared in 1961, the work of a Committee chaired by Rupert Davies and convened by Douglas Hubery. It began by admitting that in a decade the number of children in Methodism had nearly halved from one million in 1950. In 1953 there were 815,952 children, in 1960 587,276. Youth club numbers were up, but so was the number of teenagers in the population. Was Methodism, then, a dying church? [66]

At the time, Emil Brunner's dictum, 'The Church took a wrong turning when it substituted the technique of the classroom for the technique of the community in religious education,' was repeatedly quoted.[1] By baptism, it was stressed, children were part not of the church of tomorrow but of the church of today, and their place in the worshipping community was vital.

---

**65.** 1. The first task of the Sunday School is to introduce a child and retain him (sic!) in the worshipping and teaching atmosphere and tradition of the Christian church. This assumes infant baptism and its follow up.

2. The second task is to help its members to feel that they are an integral part of a community which cares for them as individuals and demands and values their loyalty.

3. The third task is the deliberate development of every child committed to it as a whole person and a spiritual being with numerous powers within the Christian community. It should quicken a child's interest in a knowledge of music and poetry and art . . . it should encourage him in the proper attitude, at the various stages of his physical and emotional development, to the members of the opposite sex.

4. The fourth task is the teaching of the Christian faith. This involves every possible mode of communication, not least personal friendship.

5. The fifth task is to bring its members to the point of decision for Christ and of accepting the grace of God which is offered them in Christ. Evangelism and education are thus partners.

6. The sixth task is that of bringing into the full membership of the Christian church those who by the act of faith and decision have received the grace of pardon through Jesus Christ. To be in Christ is to be in the church.

7. The seventh task is to continue the training and to assist the growth of those who have entered full membership of the church.

*Source*: R. E. Davies, *The Sunday School Today*, Methodist Youth Department 1951, pp. 1–17, summarized.

---

**66.** The Commission recommends that serious consideration should be given to the forms of service used when children share in the Worship of the Church. It is important that they be enabled to participate fully in the adoration, thanksgiving, confession, petition and intercession of the church, and in the hearing of the Scriptures before going to their separate departments. It is less important that the children should listen to a children's address, the value of which is open to doubt.

*Source*: *The Way Ahead*, Methodist Youth Department 1961, p. 20.

At the same time, the category of 'Junior Members' was abolished as an anomaly, being replaced by the concept of 'members in training', which pointed forward to public reception into church membership at an appropriate time. The report emphasized the need for adequate training of all those working among children and young people, a matter underlined in the handbook *Preparation for Service* (1972).[2] The fact, however, that, granted the contemporary swing to morning Sunday School, the minister often had little rapport with children unless he addressed them directly in church was unfortunately forgotten. As a result, scholars like Gordon Rupp began to deplore the fact that young people tended to be 'withdrawn' from preaching and sacrament alike, with dire psychological consequences.

The 'caring church' was another slogan, alongside stress on the follow-up to baptism, the proper training of helpers, new styles of educational methods, teachers' fellowships, the guidance of a properly trained minister, much more integration of Sunday School work and mid-week activities, and use of the *School Hymn Book of the Methodist Church* (1951). This book – fine, if a little 'highbrow', though it was – was increasingly becoming out of touch with the materials used in many day schools. 'Family Worship' (as it was then called, in the wake of the thinking of H. A. Hamilton of Westhill College)[3] was to be encouraged at the festivals. Because, however, Sunday Schools still tended to be held in the afternoon, the 'Family Service' in many churches was more often a 'parade service', involving uniformed organizations and considerable numbers of teenagers. Since the 1960s the average age has gone down, and consequently a different style of worship is now normally offered.

The Free Church Federal Council reports stressed the confusion between Day School RI (and for some it was still 'Religious Instruction', evolving into 'Religious Knowledge', then 'Religious Education', and now often 'Religious Studies', each title indicating a different educational concept) and Sunday School. Archbishop Garbett's claim that 'the future of religion in this country now largely depends on the way in which it is both taught and practised in Day Schools'[4] was taken very seriously. Partnership between church, home and school was stressed. All this clearly reflected the concept behind the clauses about religion in the Education Act of 1944, but in an increasingly pluralistic society, which saw religious education as purely an exploration of religion as a part of human life, allegiance to the claims of church, synagogue or mosque was soon treated as a matter of personal choice rather than state responsibility. The West Riding Syllabus of 1966, *Suggestions for Religious Education*, in which a Methodist, Alan Loosemore, played an important role, is a fine example of the thinking of those days. The changes since then have been enormous, as a glance at successive syllabuses – for example, in Birmingham – will reveal.

The 1960s saw great changes in the style of official Methodist Sunday School material, the influence of educationalists like R. J. Goldman being welcomed by Douglas Hubery (1916–88), later to be General Secretary of the Division of Education and Youth, Dr H. F. Mathews, Clifford Jones and others.[5] The rather stolid didactic style of the 1940s and 1950s was rapidly replaced by 'experiential' material, which stressed relating to children's experience rather than 'telling the Christian story'. (Interestingly, 'the story' approach came back into fashion in the 1980s both in educational circles and in the pulpit.) The style which attempted to enable children to grasp the Bible's story was replaced by thematic material geared to each age group. This practice presupposed the psychological theories of Piaget, mediated by Goldman, which stressed the movement of children from 'preconceptual' through 'intuitive' to 'concrete' thinking (the Junior Age) and on to 'abstract' or formal thinking in adolescence. Sadly, at this point, some Methodist churches ceased to use 'official' Methodist literature, such as the New British Lessons Council Syllabus *Experience and Faith* (1968) together with the Partners in Learning material based on it. They preferred more 'biblically based' teaching aids, better geared – to put it frankly – to the less sophisticated teacher. It was thought that Goldman had implied that the Bible, and especially the Old Testament, was to be largely used at the 'abstract' or formal thinking stage – in other words, that it was a book for adults and not for children. Whatever the advantages of the new approach, there can be little doubt that what was seen as uncritical denigration of older teaching methods produced a resurgence, in some churches, of an even more old-fashioned fundamentalism. At the same time or a little later, some advocated 'integrated learning' as a pattern for 'All-Age Worship', thus contradicting the approach of Archibald and Hayes a generation before. Clearly, if children only worshipped with children, they would easily think that worship itself was a childish thing, to be tossed aside at adolescence. There was also an unfortunate divergence between Partners in Learning and the Joint Liturgical Group Lectionaries which, despite frequent requests, has never been entirely resolved. At several points here, liturgists and educationalists clearly disagree, though both now support baptized children sharing in the eucharist.

The British Council of Churches' report *The Child in the Church* (1976) represents well the thinking of the 1960s and early 1970s [67]. The hopes of educationalists like Spencer Leeson and documents like the Lindsey Syllabus,[6] stating that religious instruction in schools should 'increasingly lead pupils to become and remain full members of a worshipping community outside the school' are dashed. Such an approach can now only be used in 'church' schools.

---

67. The specific tasks of Christian nurture are for the church itself to undertake. The crisis in Christian nurture is thus heightened by the fact that the church and the school can no longer be thought of as partners in Christian nurture ... Secular education is to do with becoming a reflective person; Christian nurture is to do with becoming a Christian person.

*Source*: *The Child in the Church*, British Council of Churches 1976, pp. 10, 21.

---

Very little is said about evangelism's place in Christian nurture and witness, the impression being given that the church is an 'escalator', off which,

frankly, most of the baptized will later jump! There is not a little muddle here, due to rapid changes in educational theory. When I began to work as a minister in 1956, we were told 'children should be taught at their level', then there was Goldman and endless 'themes' and 'projects' exploring primary school 'topics', and now the talk is of integration and 'all-age' worship and activity.

The latest important ecumenical report *Unfinished Business. Children and the Churches* (Council of Churches for Britain and Ireland [CCBI]1995), while frowning on any direct evangelism or preaching, which is denigrated as 'standing on a soapbox', stresses the task of telling the all-important Christian story. Here Westerhoff replaces Goldman. He speaks of 'experienced faith' (the basic trust of the young child), 'affiliative faith' (sharing in the life of the family and other groups), 'searching faith' (the questioning of the adolescent as self-identity emerges), and 'owned faith' (where a person comes to own what they believe). Within such a framework, liturgy, the Christian Year and the sacraments, not to mention evangelism, can clearly have an honoured and significant place.

In the present situation, however, there are ominous facts which cannot be ignored. Sadly, the age of innocence has gone, and the child is now the 'adult child'. He or she is often part of a one-parent household. The percentage of the UK's population living in so-called traditional family units – married parents with dependent children – has declined from 52% in 1961 to 40% in 1992. One child in four will experience the divorce of parents before the age of sixteen. Between 1979 and 1993 the proportion of children living in families receiving below 50% average income increased from 1 in 10 to nearly 1 in 3. While 'relative deprivation' figures need cautious use, there is no room for complacency. Meanwhile only 15% of children have any direct contact with the churches, and about 80% of these are from church backgrounds.

Against such a background, the question of recruitment to Sunday Schools and other such activities within the church's life inevitably causes nagging worries. Do the sects do better, we ask ourselves, than the mainstream churches? And if so, why? For the moment, *Unfinished Business*, though sometimes a little romantic – it speaks of children as potential 'prophets' or 'priests' rather than as people to be loved, nurtured, disciplined and taught – rightly stresses the role of children in the church community [68].

> **68.** A church which welcomes children, accepts their gifts and ministries, meets their needs, advocates justice, seeks new life, challenges evil with love and truth, and continues to learn the values of the Kingdom by living them, is a church which is good news not only for its members but for the world.
>
> *Source*: *Unfinished Business*, CCBI 1995, p. 62.

So far in this chapter, we have attempted to express the confusion and even the agony sometimes experienced at the 'grassroots' as churches have tried to be faithful in work with children. We end with a question, well worth pondering. Why is it that, although the Partners in Learning series now provides a fine modern teaching aid for Junior Churches, they are much less used than the old 'Methodist Notes', in which biblical scholars and theologians like the late Norman Snaith added their expertise to that of the educationalists?

## 2. Uniformed organizations

Many Methodist churches have uniformed organizations – Girls Brigade and Boys Brigade with their younger groups like the Anchor Boys and the less church-dominated Scouts and Guides, with Cubs and Brownies. Through such groups, which have withstood the changes of recent years reasonably well, links can be built with families right outside the church. The enormous amount of work involved in this kind of activity, however, is often barely acknowledged, and shortage of leaders is a great problem. Perhaps the Boys Brigade, helped by the very progressive Hayes Report of the early 1960s, has had most success in reaching boys outside the normal church set-up and bringing numbers of them into full Christian discipleship. Denigrated by some, who sniffed militarism behind every bugle, these groups have shown, often more than Sunday Schools, a remarkable capacity to survive.

## 3. Schools and colleges

The contribution of Methodism at every educational level is not a matter of triumphalism, but of proper pride. Westminster College (first in London, later after the Second World War at Oxford), originally a training college for teachers and now much wider in its scope, and Southlands College, Wimbledon (now part of the Roehampton Institute) have been notable. Among their outstanding Principals were the distinguished historians Herbert Workman and Archibald Harrison, the latter having a key role as Free Church Negotiator in the consultations leading to the Education Act of 1944. The calibre of the teachers trained to enter state schools at a time when the prestige of teachers as role models was very important constitutes a remarkable achievement. The sociologist David Martin said that the central figure for teaching Christianity is a lady in a primary school! By a happy chance for Christianity, those who teach in primary schools show greater sympathy and commitment to the faith than most social groupings.

The complex of Methodist Day Schools – 900 at its maximum – is now very small, 28 mainly in Lancashire and another 28 now ecumenical. The great rise in the professional classes saw Methodism produce a chain of public schools comparable with the Woodard schools associated with the Anglo–Catholic Movement. These were added to Kingswood School, founded by John Wesley himself, and Woodhouse Grove School at Bradford. Many people distinguished in public life well outside the traditional Methodist orbit owed much to these schools. The late Sir Geoffrey Elton, for example, Regius Professor of History at Cambridge, was at Rydal School after fleeing, with his mother and his brother, from the

Nazis. Outstanding in educational circles was A. B. Sackett, who was headmaster at Kingswood School from 1928 to 1959. Schools of this kind produced people of integrity, not all of whom remained Methodist – the historian E. P. Thompson, son of a missionary, can serve as an example.

Opinion is divided in Methodism about the morality of sponsoring independent schools. Certainly fewer Methodists now attend them than was the case in the immediately pre-war period, and far fewer ministerial families are now involved than in the days when, granted the movement of ministers every three years, boarding education offered welcome continuity for ministers' children.

Methodists have played notable roles in state schools. At my old school, Wolverhampton Grammar school, it provided headmasters of the calibre of Warren Derry (1929–56), close friend and biographer of Sackett, Ernest R. Taylor (1956–71) and Anthony Stocks (1971–76). None of these men were narrowly denominational, let alone sectarian, but gave an example of intellectual and educational integrity which was incalculably valuable to the large numbers whom they influenced. Here was a breadth of life with a clear Christian but undogmatic educational style. Clearly much of this contribution to education can be paralleled in all the churches, especially in the period after 1945, when there was an interesting resurgence of Christian faith, with outstanding exponents. In Cambridge, testified C. S. Lewis, it was more normal to be Christian than it had been for a generation or so. The reasons for the subsequent decline are exceedingly complex and include a rejection of the Enlightenment as well as of orthodox Christianity in a curiously irrational post-modernism.

## 4. Youth clubs

In 1995 the Methodist Association of Youth Clubs (MAYC) celebrated its fiftieth birthday. It was a product of the Second World War and of new thinking, in religious and secular circles, about the needs of young people. In 1943 the Methodist Youth Department (now the Division of Education and Youth) was created under the leadership of J. K. Whitehead (1893–1984), Bryan Reed (1905–91) and Douglas Griffiths (1898–1982). The earlier pioneer of youth clubs was Jimmy Butterworth (1897–1977), whose concept and practice at 'Clubland' in Camberwell, East London provided a remarkable model. The motto of the Methodist Youth Department [69], though a little dated now, still has a Methodist ring about it.

---

69.
1. In life devoted
2. In faith equipped
3. In person fit
4. In church a family
5. In service world citizens

*Source*: *The Charter Explained*, MYD.

---

MAYC was more varied in style than Butterworth's model. It met a particular need when large numbers of young people were 'clubbable' and, if there was good leadership available, as there often was, enjoyed a corporate activity. The London Weekends,[7] which quickly became a feature of MAYC, were not only highly professional but enormous fun, not least when, before the whole enterprise became much more sophisticated, the participants had to sleep in the underground shelters. Douglas Griffiths was the key ministerial figure in the early days with Leonard Barnett and Reginald Bedford (1916–88) to follow. Worship on these occasions was remarkably exuberant and inspirational. It was important for young people to feel that they were part of something big. But in the end it was youth leaders, like Philip Race in Lincoln and Harold Emms in Colchester, who were the key people.

A typical early club was the Questors of Beckminster, Wolverhampton, founded in 1943 and linked immediately with MAYC. The early programmes of social evenings, hikes, holidays, country dancing ('ballroom' dancing was still frowned upon!), devotional sessions and Sunday worship may seem rather 'tame' now, but it was immensely popular then. In different forms that club still flourishes, participating in all the many MAYC fundraising activities for Third World need. The great days of MAYC were the 1950s and 1960s, and Victoria Street, Burton upon Trent, under Ray Fisher, was typical of the well-run youth club. The area was very much innerbelt, its young people often having problems. But thanks to good discipline and splendid, caring leadership, the impact on a tough neighbourhood was remarkable. With club nights, club services in a church prepared to take risks in worship – a woman preacher was once amazed to be given a prolonged round of applause! – a club squash at the Manse and, as with Questors, club holidays and youth weekends with open evangelism, this was equally remote from vague liberalism and fundamentalism. Ministers were able (with lay collaboration) to run training classes for 'full church membership', as it was then called. Not a few youngsters remained firmly with the church. There were links with the wider national association of young girls and mixed clubs, with Sir Harold Hayward (a member at Victoria Street in his younger days) a very valuable Methodist link person. Here was Methodism's evangelism-by-friendship at its best.

Changes in youth work came with the 1960s' Albermarle Report[8] and, consequently, greater liaison with local authorities. The older clubs, like Questors or Culver Street, Colchester, were entirely church supported. As many churches began to co-operate with the LEAs, however, a more varied type of youngster joined, trained and paid leaders were used, and a much more 'secular' programme emerged. King Cross Church, Halifax was typical. A large club was led in the 1970s by Miss Enid Bamforth, who had in her kitchen two large knives grabbed when she dived in to stop two lads stabbing each other! None of these youngsters came into the worshipping life of the church, though later, when coming for weddings and baptisms, many testified to the leaders' influence on them. Years afterwards, in the 1980s, leaders tended to be swamped by more aggressive, 'unclubbable' youngsters. The club was wrecked. The LEA withdrew its support. As a result, a youth fellowship of church-based youngsters was developed, and is growing. The wheel comes full circle, that particular saga

expressing the changes from 1945 to 1990. Now the church is having to develop its own independent work again, with less LEA support, if any. MAYC still has a vital role in the life of Methodism [70]. One way of enabling Methodists today to live on a large map is exemplified by the mixture of urgency and idealism in the proposals presented by young people in 'Charter 95'.[9]

---

70. *Seven Principles of MAYC:*

1. Create a cell.
2. Grow real persons.
3. Grow a sense of belonging.
4. Develop a balanced programme.
5. Go for the first rate.
6. Live on a large map.
7. Take your place in the church.

*Source: Seven Guiding Principles of MAYC Clubs*, Methodist Youth Department 1956.

---

## 5. University Methodist societies

We now turn to a fascinating sociological phenomenon. In the 1930s there was an increase in the number of children from Methodist families entering higher education. Adrian Hastings has shown the same pattern in Roman Catholicism.[10] He writes of a 'relaxed chaplaincy system' and a general diminishing of prejudice against the vastly enlarged Catholic pressure in the universities. He speaks, too, of the emergence of an intelligentsia in Catholic circles, which can be paralleled in Methodism. If Cambridge had the Catholic David Knowles, 'the noblest English Catholic historian since Acton', he was matched by his friend the Methodist Herbert Butterfield who had 'head hunted' him for Peterhouse.

In Cambridge Harold Beales (1886–1967) was minister of Wesley Church in 1930. Building on the contemporary theology of experience, he began to explore with Methodist students what faith could mean and how it could be communicated. Young 'dons' like Butterfield and Charles Coulson (later at

London and Oxford) and theological students at Wesley House had a positive influence on undergraduates. Role models are of greater significance than is sometimes realized by those who seem to denigrate the effect of first-rate teachers and exemplars. At Oxford, a parallel was the pastorate of Harold Roberts (1896–1982), who in 1930 had twenty-eight students in the John Wesley Society. He enabled them to find a vibrant faith which produced leaders of the calibre of Rupert Davies, Mary Lenton, Margaret Holt (later Mrs Rupert Davies) and Raymond George. Many students were enabled to explore the faith and equipped to meet the demands of the next four decades, even if they did not remain Methodists [71].

---

71. I was the first Roberts to get to Oxbridge. I knew my parents were proud of it . . . I joined a Methodist study group which held tea parties for which my mother would send me cakes through the post. Religion figures large in my Oxford life. Many young people enter university and lose their faith but I never felt any danger of that. Methodism provided me with an anchor of stability as well as friends, who looked at the world as I did.

*Source*: Margaret Thatcher, *The Path to Power*, Harper-Collins 1995, pp. 37–40.

---

The Methodist chaplain at Oxford at that time was Frederic Greeves, of whom a fellow student, the future historian W. R. Ward, said: 'It came as something of a surprise to find a man talking of Christianity from the pulpit as an intelligent man might.'[11] Greeves himself reflected: 'The outstanding instance of great progress in contemporary Methodism is provided by the Methodist Societies in the universities. As one who spent a considerable part of his life in touch with these societies when they were emerging from small beginnings, I am convinced that some of the lessons which they can teach are not being sufficiently widely learnt.'[12] The 'MethSoc' idea spread. At London the work was centred at Hinde Street, where it later had a fine period of growth under E. R. Richardson, Arnold Cooper and Arthur Shaw. Brunswick, Leeds, became a notable centre for Leeds University and later Leeds

Polytechnic, and subsequently the work was centred at Oxford Place and Emmanuel. Cambridge MethSoc reached great strength under the ministries of Ronald Spivey, Donald Rose and Whitefield Foy, who had himself served at Brunswick. The heart of the Meth-Socs was the pastoral group for study, prayer and action, and the action included conducting worship and helping churches through missions in vacations. In the early 1950s the number of students in the MethSoc was often as large as any society in the university. In 1952, for example, Cambridge MethSoc had more groups than there are letters of the alphabet! The contribution of such groups to the wider church, lay and ministerial, has been remarkable. But there were possible snags in this style of work [72].

---

72. Cambridge University Methodist Society 1950–55 . . . was an experience of spiritual enrichment which spilled over into other parts of my life and influenced me profoundly. The weekly cycle of church services, social activity, discussion and yet more discussion . . . conducted earnestly and vigorously and with enormous good humour determined for me the rhythm of Cambridge term time. I can never forget the thrill of inspired preaching in Wesley Church or the animation with which the intricate process of planning for group events was conducted or the revelatory meditations on points of theology, especially as we ambled along the Backs on spring mornings . . . Above all I am thankful that Methodism aroused in me a deep sense of fun . . . I sometimes recall with embarrassment the naïve way in which we approached relationships between the sexes . . . I came to find 'MethSoc' less satisfying in its social gospel than in its personal relationships . . . I concluded sadly that the church itself had been moved away from me.

*Source*: R. A. Buchanan, Director of the Centre for the History of Technology, Science and Society, University of Bath, *Methodist Recorder*, 12 November 1991.

---

Even accepting such criticism, however, there was no need for membership of a thriving MethSoc to breed religious isolationism. Indeed, many, by an astute use of time, were able to take part in the activities of the Student Christian Movement (SCM) or Inter-Varsity Fellowship (IVF, now UCCF) and to participate in the life of Oxbridge college chapels. There was certainly a feeling in those post-war years that Christianity was a vibrant religion and Methodism a part of the universal church to be proud of. It is a tragedy of the highest magnitude that the impetus of the 1950s was lost, for reasons which are not entirely clear. For a church which cannot communicate an intelligible and defensible faith to those who, having passed through higher education, shape the opinions of the nation, is unlikely to make much impact on a largely secular, pluralist society with no clear moral norms. Numbers in Higher Education are now greater than ever, numbers of committed Christians smaller. But it is not only religious groups which have moved to what Grace Davie, a sociologist at Exeter University, has recently described as 'believing not belonging' or to adhering to sectarian groups or 'one interest' agencies such as those concerned with the environment.[13]

The gradual decline in the late 1960s and 1970s of the Student Christian Movement, which had been a spearhead of evangelism, was very sad indeed. The number of university teachers who are Christian, let alone Methodist, has diminished. The immense prestige of scientists like Charles Coulson at Oxford and later Russell Hindmarsh in Newcastle has never quite been repeated. It is a paradox that, while the number of students soared after the Robbins Report,[14] the number in MethSocs, despite the notable co-ordinating work of Douglas Brown, did not keep up. Today the more conservative evangelical bodies seem to attract students who, in an earlier generation, would have found the MethSoc attractive. There are subtle reasons for an increase of a more conservative style in religion, but it is clear that a somewhat dogmatic style can give some students an anchor point they might otherwise lack. The danger, of course, is a ghetto mentality – from which Methodism itself has not been entirely free!

## 6. The Wesley Guild

But what has Methodism to offer young adults past the youth club or MethSoc age? The Wesley Guild, now a hundred years old, was a very typical Methodist response to the need, at the turn of the century, for a wider style of spirituality. How could the church attract its young people and provide a viable counter-culture? Dinsdale Young, later to be a renowned preacher at Central Hall, Westminster, feared that the church would move into the entertainment business or become an excursion agency! Later, however, he supported W. B. Fitzgerald, who began the Wesley Guild in Leeds, with George Allen and Alfred Robinson to follow him [73].

> 73. Wesley Guild is a young people's society closely linked to the church, holding weekly or periodic meetings, for devotional, literary or social purposes. Its later motto was 'One Heart, One Way', with the four C's of Comradeship, Consecration, Culture and Christian service.
>
> *Source*: W. Leary, *Wesley Guild, The First Hundred Years*, The Wesley Guild 1995, pp. 8, 16 (paraphrased).

The Guild represented a balanced style of Christian nurture, whose fruits included the Ilesha Hospital in Nigeria, which gave focus to missionary concern, and the creation of Wesley Guild Holiday Centres, which had a very wide popular appeal both to families and single people. In the 1960s, the Guild came under some criticism. It needed new life-blood and new styles and had a middle-aged air about it. In a wise church it could still be an important part of a balanced church programme. Young adults and middle-aged people need a meeting ground with a varied programme. A thousand branches of the Guild still remain. There are signs of a renaissance of the Guild, alongside the whole movement of house groups and informal fellowship and the occasional weekend and annual events of highly organized evangelism, education and celebration, like Easter People.[15]

## 7. Other agencies and activities

We must not forget the many attempts to meet the needs of all ages. Methodist International Houses

(MIH) are a notable way of helping students from overseas. At the other end of the age scale – and the number of over sixties in the population is growing – two organizations merit mention. Methodist Homes For the Aged (MHA) cares for over 2,000 people in residential homes and sheltered housing and is seeking to develop care for those suffering from various forms of dementia. The Methodist Local Preachers' Mutual Aid Association (LPMAA) began as a typical Victorian mutual aid society for Local Preachers in situations of poverty. With the coming of the Welfare State, a change was made to the provision of accommodation for aged Local Preachers and their spouses. 'Local Preachers' here includes those from the Wesleyan Reform and other independent styles of Methodism. Five residential homes are currently available.

Lastly, we return to work among young people. The Methodist Missionary Society has provided powerful stimulus to children not to be parochial in their interests and attitudes but to 'live on a large map' through what is now Junior Mission for All (JMA), which supports both mission at home and work in partnership with indigenous churches overseas. The Methodist Relief and Development Fund (MRDF), which responds to emergency needs worldwide, should also be mentioned in this context. All these activities and agencies suggest a church sometimes baffled by change, as we have seen in our analysis of work with children, but still able to live on a large map, in the spirit of the following prayer.

> Lord of the Years,
> help us to recognize and respond
> to your love in every season of our life:
> the spring of childhood,
> the summer of youth and adulthood,
> the autumn of our maturity
> and the winter of our age.
> We rejoice in your grace sufficient for each day.
> We praise you for the past
> and trust you for the future.
>
>                                    Amen[16]

## For discussion

1. What, if anything, did Sunday School mean for you?
2. Are Rupert Davies' points about the tasks of a Sunday School valid? If not, why not?
3. Why do you think we have now so few children outside church families in many of our suburban 'Junior Churches'?
4. How can we encourage all-age worship and at the same time enable children to enjoy being children?
5. Were the changes of the 1960s in work among children beneficial or confusing, or both?
6. What role do you think Youth Clubs now have?
7. How can churches and local authorities co-operate?
8. What co-operation with Day Schools now exists, apart from ministers conducting assembly? What links does your church have?
9. What future is there for the Wesley Guild?
10. Am I right to stress the importance of Methodist Societies on our university and college campuses?
11. What does your church do for young adults?
12. Is it good to have various kinds of Methodist homes for the aged or is this approach rather limiting?

# 9
# Methodist Scholarship

## 1. Liberal Evangelicalism

At the time of Methodist Union in 1932, Methodist theologians were much concerned with religious experience in the widest sense, evaluating it in the light of recent developments in psychology. William James' The *Varieties of Religious Experience* (1902), with its famous division of people into the 'once born' and the 'twice born', was enormously influential, and in Methodism Maldwyn Hughes' *The Theology of Experience* (1913) and C. Ryder Smith's *The Christian Experience* (1926) were typical of the approach. A fine final book in this genre came from the lay educationalist and former Primitive Methodist, Victor Murray. In *Personal Experience and the Historic Faith* (1939), Murray showed how feeling, knowing, choosing, doing and belonging are essentials of full Christian experience.[1]

Methodist biblical scholarship began to be taken seriously by a wider theological world through the linguistic studies of W. F. Moulton and his son, James Hope Moulton, and through the broader critical but constructive work of A. S. Peake, a Primitive Methodist layman who was Rylands Professor at Manchester University until his death in 1929. J. H. Moulton's death – he died in an open boat after the ship on which he had been returning from India had been torpedoed – was a great loss, not least because of his potential contribution in another sphere, as an expert on Zoroastrianism and an explorer of the relationship between Christianity and other faiths (see especially his *Religions and Religion*

1913). Peake, almost single-handed, prevented a repetition in Britain of the grievous divisions between Protestant Christians which opened up in America in the debate over the authority of the bible and evolution. He was able to combine rigorous critical scholarship, epitomized by the famous *Commentary* which he edited in 1919, with an acute but warm evangelical style of preaching.

Methodist scholars, especially those teaching in theological colleges, have usually been 'middle men', standing between the front rank of scholars in the universities and the ministers and Local Preachers who need their insights in preaching and teaching. They have also, for the most part, been as much at home in the pulpit as in the lecture room. One thinks, for example, of Robert Newton Flew of Wesley House, Cambridge, cycling to fenland villages to share his faith, not least with children, and of J. H. Moulton of Didsbury College, Manchester, preaching round the branches of the Manchester Mission. Such contributions have been vitally important within Methodism, for preaching, as St Augustine and John Calvin knew, is the prime way of articulating theology for ordinary people.

This link between theology and preaching may be further illustrated from the work of J. Alexander Findlay (1880–1961) who in the 1930s communicated the liberal, evangelical view of the Jesus of history in a series of semi-popular books. The mood was optimistic, Jesus being presented as a human being who, in communion with the Father, provided a way for others into the love of God and of their fellows. This style of theology enabled a preacher of the calibre of Leslie Weatherhead to help thousands to see Jesus as a person to be trusted and obeyed in loving discipleship. The spin-off from this liberal protestant style, combining appeals to evidence and experience, was great. Certainly Findlay, like his friend Russell Maltby, was able to inspire preachers, especially Local Preachers, and his total lack of ecclesiasticism was appealing and anticipated the renewal of liberal thinking in the 1960s [74].

---

74. (a) If Jesus be but the noblest of men, we have in the Cross only the most moving of all tragedies; but if He be God, the path of disillusionment, darkening down to despair, leads us by the only way now open to us, straight into the arms of God.

(b) . . . young people charge their elders with narrowness and an exaggerated concern with the salvation of their own souls. Their religion consists, it is said, too largely in abstentions, whereas the new understanding of Jesus which has come to us in these days has taught us that He enjoyed life to the full and condemned not so much those whom our fathers called 'the giddy multitude' as the uncharitable and the narrow minded.

*Sources*: J. A. Findlay: (a) *What did Jesus Teach?*, Hodder & Stoughton 1933, p. 205. (b) *A Portrait of Peter*, Hodder and Stoughton 1935, p. 288.

---

## 2. Biblical theology

Other emphases were emerging. Wilbert F. Howard (1880–1952) at Handsworth College, Birmingham, where his colleagues W. F. Lofthouse (1871–1965), Henry Bett and Christopher North completed a formidable quartet, expounded St John's Gospel with clarity and insight for both academic and popular audiences. But we will feature Vincent Taylor (1887–1968) as the prime exemplar of new developments in biblical scholarship. Professor Adrian Hastings, who ranks him second only to C. H. Dodd among New Testament scholars in Britain in the period 1930–60, comments: 'Perhaps he slightly lacked the flair of an absolutely first class mind but the reliability and depth of his scholarship is outstanding.'[2] His *Gospel According to St Mark* (1953) has been described by Dennis Nineham as 'the great modern English commentary on the Greek text'.[3]

Taylor,[4] who gained both his PhD and DD degrees while a circuit minister, first lays the necessary groundwork of biblical scholarship. When the text is established – he wrote a later book on textual matters – he asks: What are the sources of the gospel writers? *Behind the Third Gospel* (1926), following up his earlier *Historical Evidence for the Virgin Birth* (1920), sought to show that Luke had his own major sources before he made use of Mark. A conjectural early draft called 'Proto-Luke' is put alongside Mark as sources for knowledge of the historical Jesus. Taylor then took up the challenge of what German scholars like Dibelius and Bultmann called 'form criticism'. They asked: How were the gospel materials collected and used in the early Christian communities? How did the first Christians shape the material they had in their sermons and teachings? Taylor introduced English readers to this approach, though he did not share Rudolf Bultmann's scepticism about the possibility of penetrating to the historical Jesus behind the traditions of the early church. Taylor was determined to maintain the priority of historical evidence, arguing that, after all, the apostles were not immediately carried up into heaven. If Christianity is a historical religion, then it stands or falls by the historicity of the life, teaching, death and resurrection of Jesus, even if historians will argue about what 'historicity' really implies.[5] Taylor coined the phrase 'Pronouncement stories' to characterize episodes like Mark 12.13–17, in which the opponents of Jesus show him a coin, asking if taxes are to be paid or not, and he replies: 'Give to the Emperor the things that are the Emperor's and to God the things that are God's.' Here is a story owing something to the techniques of early Christian preaching and not dissimilar, in form if not in content, to stories about Churchill which end with the Churchillian 'punchline'!

> **75.** What are we saying today about the Cross? We rightly preach Abelardian doctrine. The Cross truly reveals the love of God and by its love kindles an answering love within us. The 'classic' theory that Christ died to deliver men from sin, evil and death is specially relevant to our chaotic world.
>
> For myself I believe that the most fruitful way of conceiving the nature of Christ's passion is the view that as Son of Man Christ identified himself with sinners and offered in their name that supreme sacrifice of obedience, penitence and love which we ourselves are unable to offer but in which we can participate by faith union, sacramental union and sacrificial living.
>
> *Source*: V. Taylor, *The Apostolic Gospel*, Epworth Press 1953, pp. 11–12.

Taylor epitomizes the new mood of what came to be called 'biblical theology', stressing the unity of the biblical revelation. Having laid the foundations – *The Gospels* (1930) and *The Formation of the Gospel Tradition* (1933) became standard textbooks – Taylor then produced two trilogies on the Work of Christ and his Person.[6] It is noticeable that Methodist scholars this century have produced major works on the atonement, while Anglican theological attention has tended to be focussed upon the incarnation. The order of Taylor's work is significant. Perhaps Methodists, whether or not they know Melanchthon's famous saying about knowing Christ being equivalent to knowing his benefits, begin instinctively with the Saviour. Taylor's *Jesus and His Sacrifice* (1937) had as much influence in Anglican circles as in Methodism, since his stress on sacrifice as the heart of atonement [75] can fit in with new insights into the Holy Communion, a matter which Taylor himself acknowledged. 'The Eucharist . . . cannot lie at the circumference of Christian worship but must stand at the centre as a means whereby man approaches God and appropriates the blessings of Christ's self-offering.'[7] This view of the relationship between the cross and the eucharist has a parentage in Augustine, Luther and Charles Wesley's eucharistic hymns, as well as in Anglican writers like R. C. Moberly. It is significant, too, that later Methodists, such as Frances Young in *Sacrifice and the Death of Christ* (1975), Kenneth Grayston in *Dying We Live* (1990) and Morna Hooker in *Not Ashamed of the Gospel* (1994), though exploring the atonement in ways not used by Taylor, still stress the cross as of central importance for christology [76].

> **76.** Atonement means a conviction that God has somehow dealt with evil, with sin, with rebellion. Perhaps the nearest we can get to expressing this is to say that on the cross, God in Christ entered into the suffering, the evil, and the sin of his world; he entered the darkness and transformed it into light, into blazing glory. He took responsibility for the existence of evil in his creation; he bore the pain of it and the guilt of it; accepted its consequences into himself, and in his love reconciled his holiness to a sinful and corrupt humanity, justifying the ungodly, accepting man just as he is.
>
> *Source*: F. Young, *Sacrifice and the Death of Christ*, SPCK 1975, reissued by SCM Press 1983, p. 94.

Taylor moved from atonement to the person of the Saviour. While dodging none of the problems and acknowledging the influence of the early Christian communities, he shows that it is possible to trace at least an outline of the life of Jesus and that the way into the theology of his person is the self-emptying (*kenosis*) of the divine Word (Phil. 2.7). Taylor stressed the humanity of Jesus, warning about calling Christ God (as the World Council of Churches' basis of membership did) without affirming manhood. He had earlier made a clear distinction between forgiveness and reconciliation, the one leading to the other – a modern way of looking at justification by faith which has never adequately been followed up. The approach is in line with a whole stream of Methodist theology, though Taylor solely concerns himself with the New Testament. Even if Taylor now seems rather dated – he did not have the sharpness of Sir Edwyn Hoskyns or the breadth of C. H. Dodd or T. W. Manson – he was representative of Methodist scholarship at its best.

Where Old Testament studies are concerned, we note the contribution of Taylor's successor as Principal of Wesley College, Headingley, Leeds, Norman H. Snaith (1898–1982).[8] Snaith's edition of the Hebrew text of the Old Testament, prepared for the Bible Society, was published in 1958, the year he was President of Conference. Snaith was proud to have come from the Primitive Methodist tradition, retaining its homely style, not least in his preaching. Though he became an expert on Hebrew worship, his most characteristic book is *The Distinctive Ideas of the Old Testament* (1944). In it he pointed to the uniqueness of Hebrew religion compared with Near Eastern religion and later Hellenism, and stressed that God's covenant-love, holiness, righteousness and grace are all elements not only of the Old Testament but also of Pauline and Reformation thinking [77]. There were emphases here which later scholars have 'deconstructed'. For example, the word studies, typical of Snaith, are now out of fashion. But at the time they illuminated the originality of the prophets.

---

77. The Jews were right when they realized that the Golden Thread in scripture is the action of God the Saviour. The work of God the Saviour runs through the whole; the Bible is all concerned with what God has done. The People of God is the people whom God has 'purchased', the people whom he chose to make his own . . . the central motif of the Old Testament is the mighty work of God the Saviour . . . the whole Bible is a unity. It is a unity in the sense that it speaks from cover to cover of the Mighty Work of God the Saviour. This is where the inspiration of scripture is manifest. No other book speaks like this.

*Source*: N. H. Snaith, *The Inspiration and Authority of the Bible*, Epworth Press 1956, pp. 31ff.

---

These developments in biblical study contributed to a renewal of preaching which was biblical and very different in style from that inspired by liberal Protestantism. To understand why, we move to a consideration of the theological emphases of the period before, during and after World War Two.

## 3. Renewal of protestantism

In Cambridge Newton Flew had a growing reputation.[9] His *The Idea of Perfection* (1934) sets John Wesley's doctrine of perfect love in the context of the whole development of the idea of Christian maturity in both Catholic and Protestant spirituality. Flew was writing about matters for too long the monopoly of the more 'Catholic' wing of the church. Spirituality, the study of the whole range of the intercourse between human beings and God, was coming into a new creative phase, illustrated by the work of Anglo–Catholics like K. E. Kirk whose *Vision of God* (1931) can be seen to anticipate and stand alongside Flew's work. Flew foreshadowed developments in spirituality which were later followed up by Gordon Wakefield and Raymond George, and by Neville Ward (1915–92), whose *The Use of Praying* (1967) could claim to be the finest book on prayer written by a modern Methodist – wise, practical, judicious, and catholic in the very best sense of the word.

Flew's interests, as we have already seen, were also similar to those of the young Michael Ramsey, whose *The Gospel and the Catholic Church* (1936) was his first and probably his most important book. Flew, responding to Ramsey with *Jesus and His Church* (1938), shows greater confidence in discovering and building theologically upon the historical Jesus. Like Ramsey, Flew is in no doubt that the cross of Christ is at the heart of the apostolic proclamation of the gospel and is always viewed in the light of the resurrection. Indeed, the resurrection, to which the apostles bore witness, is the culminating fact of their gospel. These two books – note their differing views of the development of ordained ministry – point to the debates of the 1940s and 1950s. Ramsey wrote most of the report *Catholicity* (1947), which saw Protestantism as characterized by the affirmations of the eighteenth-century revival and the stress on religious experience deriving from the German theologian Schleiermacher rather than by the insights of the great Reformers. Flew and Rupert Davies (1909–94) and a formidable team of Reformation scholars, with Philip Watson (1909–83), Gordon Rupp (1910–86) and Kenneth

Grayston representing Methodism, replied in *The Catholicity of Protestantism* (1950), a polemical but scholarly exposition of the significance of the Reformation. In this way, the fruits of a fresh exploration of the theology of Martin Luther, which had been spear-headed in England by Watson, Davies and Rupp, were made more widely available. Protestantism was shown to be not so much a negative protest as a positive assertion of God's grace and human response [78]. It is interesting that Flew and Ramsey later became advocates of Methodist–Anglican union. Though Flew felt that the Anglicans failed to understand the heart of the Reformation, the later Ramsey did in fact move from the position of *Catholicity* to a much richer appreciation of the Reformation and especially of Luther.

---

**78.** Firstly, justification springs from the 'righteousness' of God which is God's tireless activity for the forgiveness and redemption of men; it is in no sense whatever evoked by man's merits or virtues. Secondly, the faith by which through grace we are justified is a lively, active, personal trust in Jesus Christ . . . By it we are forgiven; we do not *hope* to be forgiven, which is all the Catholic view of faith allows us – we *are* forgiven . . . Genuine Christian experience is thus completely objective, objective with the objectivity of the catholic Faith, and the first Christian concept is not 'experience' but 'revelation'.

*Source*: R. N. Flew and R. E. Davies (eds), *The Catholicity of Protestantism*, Lutterworth Press 1950, pp. 79, 84.

---

Methodist scholarship was broadening its scope, no doubt helped by links, through the Finch Travelling Scholarship, between Wesley House, Cambridge and German universities. In particular, there was a surge of interest in the Reformation. Gordon Rupp,[10] a former pupil of the formidable Anglican church historian Norman Sykes (1897–1961), began by showing how Lutheran ideas influenced the English Reformers, not least the martyrs of Mary's reign. He then moved to Luther, shattering the idea even held by such a responsible thinker as William Temple (and still

prone to appear now!) that Luther by his use of the 'two kingdoms' theory – God's kingdom and the earthly kingdom also under God – was responsible in the long run for Bismarck and Hitler. In brilliant and readable books like *Luther's Progress to the Diet of Worms* (1951) and *The Righteousness of God* (1953), Rupp illuminated both Luther's humanity and his basic understanding of justification by grace through faith, which later so deeply influenced John Wesley. Wesley's heart, we should remember, was 'strangely warmed', not by a revivalist preacher but by a reading of the Preface to Luther's Commentary on Paul's Letter to the Romans. A younger generation of Methodist ministers, who saw the virtue of combining a renewed Protestantism with 'high Wesleyanism' and an openness to a needy world, regarded Rupp as their guru. His erudition was concealed by a sense of humour and a lightness of touch which enabled him to appeal to every kind of congregation, from university church to village chapel. He was a striking example of the scholar-preacher who has been a feature of

---

**79.** (a) The characteristic language, forms, institutions, disciplines, which began four hundred years ago, have come to the end of their journey, as evangelical and pastoral vehicles, however imperishable their value to the trained and instructed within the household of faith.

(b) If our Gospel is to come home to an estranged humanity, it may be that the works of the Reformation must be done again, that there must be such a ferment within the church as will produce new vocabularies, new forms of worship, new institutions, forms of Christian existence as different from those we have known as our own differ from those of the Middle Ages. Such changes are not to be enterprised from an unclean itch for innovation, by those who lay irreverent, ignorant or careless hands upon an historic inheritance. They demand a Church sensitive and obedient to the creative monitions of the Holy Ghost.

*Sources*: E. G. Rupp (a) *Luther's Progress to the Diet of Worms*, SCM Press 1951, p. 107. (b) 'The Cambridge Reformers', *Cambridge Review* 25 January 1947.

Methodist life since Wesley. At the same time, Philip Watson explored the theology of both Luther and that more humanist 'Flying Dutchman' Erasmus, while Rupert Davies opened up the view of authority expressed by the great Reformers, who claimed to stand under the sovereignty of the Word, written, preached and incarnate. It can be shown that these interests reflected deep concerns about the church struggle against Hitler, reconciliation with a shattered Germany, and the renewal of Europe. Theology is never separate from history or contemporary cultural change.

Rupp, however, had no illusions that change would come [79].

## 4. Lay scholars on the frontier

Methodism has always boasted of being a lay church. What then of its lay scholars? One of them, Professor Basil Willey, described himself as an 'inveterate trespasser in fields outside my own proper enclosure, a squatter in no man's land or everyone's land', adding that he was also 'a person whose secular province is literature and who at the same time finds a religious faith indispensable to the conduct and interpretation of life'.[11] As we shall see, at least three others – a philosopher, a scientist and a historian – could have said much the same thing.

Basil Willey (1897–1973) was Professor of English at Cambridge in the heady days of F. R. Leavis, T. R. Henn and later C. S. Lewis.[12] In a series of books which have continuing value, he tackled the development of modern pre-occupations with the place of reason and experience, the nature of authority, and the character of the universe. Willey picks his way through it all with consummate skill in *The Seventeenth Century Background* (1934), *The Eighteenth Century Background* (1946), *Nineteenth Century Studies* (1948) and *More Nineteenth Century Studies* (1956), referring particularly to literature and especially to the pervasive influence of his beloved Samuel Taylor Coleridge. 'If faith today has recovered tone and confidence, it owes this largely to the work of these pioneers who compelled it to abandon many

impossible positions.'[13] Willey, like those other Methodist laymen Sir Herbert Butterfield and Professor Thomas Jessop, gave one of the famous Cambridge Divinity School series of Saturday lectures. He offered a penetrating analysis of Victorian conflicts and testified, with powerful integrity and honesty, to his own recovered faith, quoting Coleridge's famous aphorism: 'He who begins by loving Christianity better than truth, will proceed by loving his own sect or church better than Christianity and in loving himself better than all.' This apologia is continued in *Religion Today* (1969) which took up the talking points of the theological and ethical turmoil of the 1960s. Willey knew where the shoe pinched his contemporaries and understood the need for faith in a generation 'rootless, godless and lost' [80].

> 80. I had despised the church for its creeds but meanwhile my soul was perishing of cold . . . I came to see the church as the only society of people which exists for the sake of maintaining the spiritual values and disseminating them through the lives of its members . . . So I returned to church and have never regretted it – though I still keep silence over the (to me) impossible bits of the creed.
>
> *Source*: B. Willey, *Religion Today*, Adam & Charles Black 1969, p. 122.

Professor Willey gave literary help to the teams which produced the New English Bible in 1961 and the Methodist Service Book of 1975.

Thomas E. Jessop, Vice-President of Conference in 1955, was an expert in the work of the eighteenth-century philosopher George Berkeley, and for many years Professor of Philosophy at Hull. Besides his work in philosophy, he produced a fine *Introduction to Christian Doctrine* (1960) and two books on ethics, *Social Ethics, Christian and Natural* (1952) and *The Christian Morality* (1960), the latter being the Cambridge lectures already mentioned, in which he was not afraid to question Nygren's clear distinction between human and divine love – God, he said, 'prefers a loving sinner to a loveless saint'.

Better known was Charles Coulson (1910–74).[14] Like his younger contemporary Professor Russell Hindmarsh (Vice-President 1970), he would have said, 'I profess physics and I confess Christ.' He was Vice-President in 1959, and taught at Cambridge, London and finally at Oxford, ending with four text books and 350 scientific papers to his name! Two of his books on wider topics, *Science and Christian Belief* (1959) and *Science, Technology and the Christian* (1960), reached a wide audience, and he was in constant demand at schools and colleges to guide students on matters relating to the interface between science, its outworkings in technology and its effects on the human sciences. In Christian circles he was particularly skilful in showing that the scientist as well as the religious believer is a person of faith, a seeker. This reflects the newer exploratory style of science, very different from the old-timers with their 'objective' facts and no room for mystery. Coulson also warned Christians against a 'God of the Gaps'. God, he said, is either in the whole of nature or he is not there at all. He is not the ghost in the machine [81]. Coulson was filled with great hope that science would be able, through technological advance, to solve the eventual shortage of fossil fuels by the peaceful use of atomic energy. His enthusiasms here were infectious, and they keyed in with his great concern about the world's poor, typified by his chairmanship of Oxfam and involvement in the WCC. Such optimism about the peaceful use of atomic energy, alas, proved short lived – Chernobyl saw to that! Coulson's mantle as a scientific man of faith has fallen recently on John Polkinghorne, Anglican priest and former Cambridge Professor of Mathematical Physics, who has similar gifts of enthusiastic popularization.

When I went up to Cambridge in 1949, I shared lodgings with an agnostic mathematician. 'Read this, it will shake your faith,' he said, pointing to *The Origins of Modern Science 1300–1800* (1949) by Herbert Butterfield. I was able to reply 'This might shake your agnosticism,' pointing him to *Christianity and History* (1949). 'Good Lord, the same man!' Amazingly, in that same autumn *George III, Lord North and the People 1779–80* also appeared from the same pen. Butterfield was approaching the climax of his career as a historian in Cambridge.[15]

His contributions to academic history include a major study and a sparkling biography of Napoleon, the iconoclastic *The Whig Interpretation of History* (1931) which warns of the misuse of the idea of progress, the more patriotic *The Englishman and His History* (1944), *The Statecraft of Machiavelli* (1940), more on George III, including an attack on the school of Sir Lewis Namier, two books on international diplomacy, the major studies of the history of history writing, *Man on his Past* (1955) and *The Origins of History* (1981), and many articles, popular and scholarly. It was on the frontiers between what he called 'the bright empire of the theologians' and the meaning of history that he caught the eye of a wider public. Denis Healey, who testifies to Butterfield's influence, as does Noel Annan in *Our Age*, calls him one of the great Christian pessimists. Certainly Butterfield had an Augustinian streak. 'It is essential not to have faith in human nature. Such faith is a recent heresy and a very disastrous one. What history does is to uncover man's universal sin.' He warned against self-righteousness and the dangers of wars for righteousness, showing a realism about the balance of

---

81. Science and Christianity must go forward together in mutual understanding. God cannot be at the end of science, He must be at the beginning and right through it. I believe . . . that there are certain insights which are given to the poet and the artist which are not given to anyone else and without which therefore the total life of the community is impoverished. For the more we know about God the fuller and richer will our worship be. The scientist may be God's messenger. It is sin to deny him and his element of truth . . . It is my firm conviction that in proportion as we recover the sense and significance of the doctrine of the Holy Spirit, the agency of God's creative power within the universe, so we shall be able to appreciate the unity of science and faith.

*Source*: C. A. Coulson, 'Science and Religion – A Changing Relationship', *The Cassowary*, Handsworth College Magazine 1952, pp. 16–24.

power which was very germane to the crises of the 1960s. But he adds: 'It is still the case that until some act of violence occurs we do not realize that there is a problem to be solved.' If sin was universal, so were both the judgment of God – 'his formidable non-intervention' – and his promises, culminating in the Incarnation. The Christian is one 'who holds to Christ' but is ruled by no other absolutes, certainly not by state or party or ideology.[16]

*Christianity and History* and its sequels were part of the renewal of Christian thought after the war. Like Coulson and Willey, Butterfield was a liberal evangelical with a deep concern for the individual, for an 'insurgent' New Testament style of Christianity and for an affirmation of the Providence of God operating at all levels of life. The great composer, after all, does not have to wait until the last bar has been composed for the music to have meaning. Though rejecting Utopianism, Butterfield was ultimately in the Methodist tradition of the optimism of grace [82].

---

82. Secularism is very hostile to Christianity at the moment and partly for understandable reasons, but it is fickle and flexible and amorphous . . . liable to sink back into dark astrologies, weird theosophies and bleak superstitions. That no doubt is one of the reasons why Christianity found its opportunity in the ancient Roman Empire. I think that the spread of secularism offers Christianity not only its greatest test but also the greatest opportunity that it has ever had in history . . .

There is a providence in the historical process which makes it more profitable to be guided by one's faith and one's hopes than by one's fears.

*Source*: C. T. McIntire (ed), *Herbert Butterfield: Writings on Christianity and History*, OUP 1979, pp. 251, 260.

---

Taylor, Snaith, Flew, Rupp, Willey, Coulson and Butterfield reflect the breadth of Methodist thinking and also, perhaps, what William Strawson has called a middle-of-the-road style, avoiding extreme positions. What of more recent trends? In the field of practical and pastoral theology Frederic Greeves' *Theology and*

*the Cure of Souls* (1960) was important, and was followed up by Trevor Rowe at Queen's College Birmingham in the 1970s. David Pailin at Manchester has written notably on the philosophy of religion, as has Richard Jones in the field of personal and social ethics. Frances Young was not afraid to probe the real meaning of incarnation in her contribution to the controversial *The Myth of God Incarnate* (1977) but was in a long Methodist tradition in seeing theology as testimony – 'I find salvation in Christ because in him God is disclosed to me as a "suffering" God.' Much Methodist scholarship has explored our historical heritage. Frank Baker at Duke University, USA has pioneered the Bicentennial Edition of Wesley's works, while Henry Rack's *Reasonable Enthusiast: John Wesley and the Rise of Methodism* (1989) and the work of Reginald Ward and John Walsh have saved Methodism from hagiography and sentimentality. Kingsley Barrett, Howard Marshall, Morna Hooker and James Dunn have continued the Methodist contribution to biblical scholarship.

Methodist theology is basically mainstream Christian theology and, though it is possible to trace a characteristic stress on the centrality of salvation, it has always picked up the concerns of the wider church around it. Geoffrey Wainwright, now of Duke University, is entirely representative of this tradition [83], and a survey of his work will fittingly conclude this discussion. He opened up the whole debate about baptism in *Christian Initiation* (1969), following up W. F. Flemington's splendid *The New Testament Doctrine of Baptism* (1948). In 1971 he wrote *Eucharist and Eschatology* and subsequently helped to edit the very influential *The Study of Liturgy* (1978, 2nd edn 1992) and *The Study of Spirituality* (1986). His *Doxology* (1980) is a systematic theology written from the point of view of worship. It begins not at the academic's desk but in the experience of the worshipping community from the early church onwards. And here we come back to the start of this brief exploration. Methodism, seeing theology as plain truth for plain people and believing in the transformation of individuals and society, makes a distinctive contribution, free from sectarian bias. And in doing so, it holds worship and theology together. Why? Because, if a church which ceases to worship is dead, a church which ceases to think is on the way to irrelevance.

The *Epworth Review*, therefore, following the *London Quarterly and Holborn Review*, seeks to foster scholarship and exploration, and the Epworth Press, which has had its traumas in the past, is now, alongside the Methodist Publishing House, an effective unit of communication.

---

**83.** As long as this world lasts, the Church must bear witness to it of the justice and peace which she knows from the deep, abiding and definitive Kingdom of God and which should find at least a provisional, fragmentary and outward expression in the political realm.

*Source*: G. Wainwright, *The Ecumenical Moment*, Eerdmans 1983, p. 1.

---

## For discussion

1. What do you think is the role of scholars in the church? Do they do more harm than good?
2. Does it matter if we are not sure whether all the Gospel records are eye-witness accounts?
3. Modern scholars stress the diversity of the early Christian communities. Is that an enrichment of our thinking about the early church?
4. Are lay scholars more able to recognize and respond to difficulties about matters of faith than their ministerial contemporaries?
5. If you have a scientific background, does this make faith easier, harder or more exciting?
6. Can theology be done by those outside the community of believers?
7. How do we approach dialogue with people of other faiths?

# 10

# Methodism and the Future

In 1963[1] Rupert Davies set down four possible futures for Methodism:

(a) *Organic union with the English Free Churches* This option may appear more feasible than, granted recent history, it really is. In 1972 the Congregational Church and the Presbyterian Church of England came together to form the United Reformed Church, while the Baptist Union was unable to contemplate union with any church not committed to 'believers' baptism'. It is significant, however, that the disciples of Christ were later able to unite with the United Reformed Church on the basis of a formula which allowed either infant baptism or an act of thanksgiving, followed at a suitable interval by responsive baptism. Talks about possible union negotiations between Methodism and the United Reformed Church in the early 1990s came to nothing. There seems little enthusiasm for union in either church, despite shared participation in many Local Ecumenical Partnerships.

(b) *Membership of a World Methodist Church* The World Methodist Council has, from time to time, discussed the possibility of such a church. The idea, American in origin, was hardly considered in Great Britain. Americans, because of the size of their church, would inevitably dominate any world Methodist body, and British membership could be seen as desertion of neighbouring churches in these islands. The notion of a world Methodist grouping, however, has recently resurfaced as a way of supporting smaller Methodist churches in Europe.

(c) *Intercommunion, and later union, with the Church of England* We have already analysed attempts to achieve this. 'Talks about talks' with the same end in view began in 1995. No agenda has yet been drawn up, but Methodism is likely to be wary of any proposals which do not involve mutual recognition of ordained ministry. I detect little enthusiasm for another 'scheme', but local initiatives may force the pace, and, not only in England. A Working Party's Report on a possible new round of conversations came before the Anglican General Synod in late 1997, and will be presented to the Methodist Conference in June 1998.

(d) *Continuing existence as an autonomous body* Rupert Davies reckoned that, in this case, membership would decline and then level out, while worship, organization, techniques of evangelism, ways of raising money and training of the ministry would all improve. By and large, this judgment has proved to be right. Methodism has survived better than many thought possible, though, as we have seen, it possesses less theological and political influence than once it had. Whether it can fulfil a comprehensive ministry on its own is a question which we now explore.

What then separates us today from the Church of England? Doctrinal differences, it seems, are not for many, perhaps most, churchgoers a major factor. In our 'market economy' society, even the choice of a church is made after 'shopping around' for something with which folk can be 'comfortable'. The decisive characteristics can be lively worship, warm fellowship or good activities for the children. As a result, many congregations reflect a mixture of traditions, and an earnest Methodist minister, talking about 'our doctrines', can cause confusion. In this respect, our contemporary pragmatism contrasts starkly with the traditional stand which the Free Churches made, on principle, against the 'assumption of effortless superiority' associated with the establishment, past and present. It should be noted, however, that some evangelicals are stating that we are now 'post-denominational'. They clearly have a point, and it should be taken seriously. The danger in such a situation, put in Methodist terms, would be a kind of 'congregationalism' leading to a lack of any 'connexional' sense.

But may not 'establishment' itself still have value? In Scotland, of course, the established church is Presbyterian, while in Northern Ireland and Wales there is no established church and therefore, technically, no Nonconformity. In England, however, 'establishment' still tends to be linked with the parish system, on the one hand, and influence in the corridors of power, on the other.

The classic understanding of the parish system goes back to the sixteenth century when church and commonwealth (or nation) were regarded as a single entity. If you belonged to one, you belonged to the other; and the church sought to minister – and theoretically seeks to minister still – to all in every parish. This mechanism for expressing a concern 'with the whole life of society and nation' enshrines a noble concept, and at its best helps those whose religion is inarticulate and of a 'folk religion' style. In today's religiously plural society, however, it can seem patronizing, and in any case – as Archbishop Runcie acknowledged – the same openness to a needy world can be found among Roman Catholics, URCs and Methodists. Moreover – and here is a paradox indeed – resurgent evangelicalism in the Church of England, by imposing conditions for infant baptism, seems to presuppose something close to the 'gathered church' view so central to some forms of Free Church polity.

But what of ministry to those in power? 'To be close to those in power is to have first-hand knowledge of the complexity of the actual choices facing them' – and, as Lord Habgood, former Archbishop of York,

goes on to point out, this can have a devastating effect on prophetic certainties.[2] It has to be admitted, however, that during the Second World War Bishop George Bell was able, from within the establishment, to be a model of critical and creative dissent unmatched by many Free Church leaders.

Other writers – for example, Bernard Lord Manning and Daniel Jenkins from the Free Churches and Adrian Hastings from Roman Catholicism[3] – have feared that disestablishment could involve a reduction in the Church of England's range of concern. But even if it remains established, the Church of England's ability to reach the disadvantaged seems likely to be hampered, for the foreseeable future, by the continuing debate about women priests, homosexual practice, and doctrinal and liturgical diversity. At the same time, if talks between Methodism and the Church of England get under way, the possibility of a revised establishment, akin to Scotland's 'recognition without power', could well be on the agenda.

Against this background, then, let us look at nine ways in which Methodism may have an important, continuing role.

## 1. By making a contribution to a new style of ecumenism

It seems clear that, in today's world, no one denomination – whether established or not – can provide everything that is needed. In such a situation, there must be mutual trust between the churches, and a glad co-operation which makes their strengths available to the whole community [84]. In one parish, the vicar may have a concern for healing, the Methodist minister for theological exploration. Let them both work for all! Elsewhere, the black Churches or the Pentecostals or the Roman Catholics may be able to reach folk for whom the Methodists, because of their middle-class or lower middle-class social structure, have no particular appeal. Rather than feeling guilty about not reaching the entire population, Methodists should rejoice that others are able to fill the gaps in their own competence. At the same time, however, they should not neglect any human need on the grounds that others can do it better! Rather, they should do all that they can to ensure that their own contribution is part of a co-ordinated Christian effort.

---

84. If the churches are to draw together to experience and express a deepening of their communion with Christ and with one another in the church, they need:

i. to examine their respective traditions, to rediscover what it means to be the local and universal church, to examine how these traditions are actually embodied in their own churches and to renew them if necessary;

ii. to examine one another's traditions, to discuss them together and to be prepared to be enriched by one another's understandings and ways of being church;

iii. to be honest with one another and to explain what it is in other traditions that they find difficult to accept, and to be prepared to change things that offend others and can be changed.

*Source*: *Called to be ONE*, Churches Together in England 1996, p. 54.

---

## 2. By preserving their distinctive style of worship and preaching

'Christian worship', said Karl Barth, 'is the most momentous, the most urgent, the most glorious action that can take place in human life.'[4] Unfortunately, it can also be a battleground on which strong convictions struggle with each other and endanger the overall well-being of the church. Today, however, Catholic charismatics seem to balance 'enthusiasm' and high sacramentalism with some success. Perhaps their example will encourage Methodism to rise to a similar challenge – to come to terms with all-age worship without abandoning the expository, prophetic style of preaching which was once its glory. There are still people, we may be sure, who need an articulate faith not always aided by the more charismatic styles. But, to help them, preaching will need to be more varied and imaginative, and a new generation of 'wordsmiths' is desperately needed.

Where worship is concerned, it is doubtful whether the move from formal liturgies to more informal approaches or the modernization of the language used in worship have touched the heart of the matter. Over thirty years ago Henry Rack [85] pointed to the complexity of the issues posed.

---

85. It cannot be assumed . . . that the recovery of the purity of primitive liturgy will somehow bring people back to worship with a fresh interest. For reasons which we are, perhaps, only beginning to understand, the old symbols have ceased to convince and to move, and for psychological and social reasons it is doubtful whether either the Cranmerian prayers or modern appeals to the family spirit express the needs and aspirations of people today. What is needed is not only flexibility and experiment in forms of worship but also a more searching analysis of what public prayer and worship should express.

*Source*: H. D. Rack: *The Future of John Wesley's Methodism*, Lutterworth Press 1965, p. 77.

---

Have the relevant responses been forthcoming? There are certainly signs in Methodism of a much more imaginative approach to Holy Communion, and co-operation between the leader and the congregation in the preparation of worship is increasingly common. Moreover, by these developments, time consuming though they may be, people are being helped not only to perceive what worship is about but also to 'own' it for themselves. Such approaches, however, may be much less exciting than the exuberant styles, found in some quarters, whose exponents would claim that they are more in touch with the post-modernist taste for the immediate, the tactile, the visual and the emotional all at once. In such complex circumstances, it is important never to forget that the search for Christian perfection, which lies at the heart of the Methodist tradition, must always concentrate on promoting personal maturity.

All in all, then, while the benefits of shared exploration must be acknowledged, there is still a place for a form of worship with an evangelical edge, a relevance to those new to the church and a concern for those who need to grow in faith – and Methodism could still develop it.

## 3. By always taking a wide view of the use of Christian resources

Can Methodism make a conscious attempt to mobilize Christian resources? For thirty years or more, it has seemed imperative that Christians with common concerns – doctors, social workers, teachers, political leaders – should meet in groups across denominational barriers to discuss issues and formulate policies [86]. But this has not happened as some hoped that it might. Is there a similar need, not yet addressed, to tap theological resources? It appears that there is, and that Methodism is well equipped, thanks to its connexional structures, to take important initiatives, not least at District level. At present, despite Churches Together, much time certainly seems to be wasted by denominations working independently. And it would be sad to assume that so-called 'liberals' within the churches are less willing to support such 'living on a large map' than so-called 'evangelicals'. Common witness and service to the world needs a much sharper emphasis in the next decade.

## 4. By developing theological education at all levels of church life

We have already stressed the importance of work in youth clubs and college and university Methodist societies. The urgent need for theological education across the board can be underlined by considering the needs of young adults, particularly those sitting loose to church life. They may find our worship styles unhelpful, but their hesitations about the church have other, perhaps deeper, roots. Is it possible, they ask, to challenge the values of our day without falling into what they perceive as the negative self-righteousness of the past? In their uncertainty about this, they tend to join groups with a single, powerful concern like Friends of the Earth or Oxfam or Amnesty International. Can the church, they also ask, combine exuberant enthusiasm with hard-headed wrestling with the major problems about faith and life which beset us? To this question they await a clear answer – and here is the challenge and opportunity. In other words, Methodism faces a double task: on the one

---

86. 'We get so little opportunity to hammer things out as Christians.' (Doctor)

'What I'm after is an obligation on laity to explain how they're operating as Christians. There ought to be a requirement laid on me to say what I'm up to.' (Headmaster)

'If we are going to survive as a church the emphasis has simply got to be on what unites us and *not* on what divides us.' (Councillor)

It is the laity as a whole who remain the indispensable source of leadership for a New Missionary Movement in the years ahead. Each diocese, district or area could render an invaluable service by seeking in every way possible to encourage suitable lay men and women to prepare for this role.

*Source*: David Clark, *The Liberation of the Church*, National Centre for Christian Communities and Networks 1984, pp. 44, 175, 180.

---

87. Why do so many of us seem to be ashamed of being the kind of specialist that we are supposed to be? When a minister or Christian lay worker says 'I'm not interested in theology', we should perhaps do him the courtesy of treating his comment as a jest. But what kind of joke should we think it to be if a pilot remarked 'I'm not interested in aeronautics' or if a doctor told us, as we entered his surgery 'Of course, medicine is not my line.' It is essential that every Christian who cares for his neighbours should seek such understanding as a layman can acquire of all that is being done by those who professionally serve the mental and physical needs of mankind; and it need hardly be added, in so far as Christians participate in those professional services they are as truly serving their Lord as is any minister of religion or lay pastoral worker. But even if we hesitate to speak of theology as a science, we need to rediscover the truth that the Christian ministry is a profession as well as a vocation.

*Source*: F. Greeves, *Theology and the Cure of Souls*, Epworth Press 1960, p. 26.

hand, to foster a theologically articulate ordained ministry, men and women who are 'folk theologians', helping the people of God to meet the realities of life with an informed and alert faith [87]; on the other, to develop and maintain our theological colleges as centres of excellence where lay people can find, thanks to ecumenical co-operation, the resources they need. The difficulties are not to be underestimated, but so important a project should not be beyond the capacity of a church with an unbroken concern for education of all kinds, reaching back to John Wesley!

## 5. By telling our nation the truth about itself, by word and deed

The Division of Social Responsibility within the Methodist Church has produced fine leaders and fine reports but has sometimes been hindered by the tendency of the Methodist Conference to pass Notices of Motion which are superficial and ill-conceived. There is, therefore, a constant need to ask whether we are, for example, effectively helping our young people to find vocations in local government, industry, commerce and politics as well as in teaching, the health service and the great caring professions. As we look at church history, we see the role of what some in the 1960s called 'Abrahamic communities' – that is, groups prepared to go out, like Abraham, not knowing where they were to go 'save in faith'. In Methodism we have had the National Children's Home, the Wesley Deaconess Order, and Katharine Price Hughes' Sisters of the People. More recently, paralleling Iona or Corymeela, we can point to the Ashram Communities, pioneered by Dr John Vincent, whose constant pleas for 'inner city colonies' or 'new style friars or nuns' pledged to poverty [88] still merit attention. The ecumenical possibilities of the work of all these groups need to be explored more. But where are the takers? It is heartening that Professor Robin Gill[5] pleads for 'prophetic individuals' or 'prophetic communities' rather than conference resolutions. The challenge today is to show the entrepreneurial spirit which fuelled the exploits of Thomas Bowman

Stephenson (founder of the National Children's Home) and John Scott Lidgett (founder of the Bermondsey Settlement) as the twentieth century dawned.

---

88. More probably, the hope of a People's Church lies in a new inter-denominationalism or post-denominationalism. Perhaps we may see ecumenical task forces, orders of friars/sisters, people's preachers or lay evangelists. The new-style churches of the last two decades, the black Pentecostal churches and the House Church Movement might even show the way. Certainly twenty years in the inner city makes me long for a new movement in Christianity – of the people, for the people, led by the people. And confronting the existing churches with another kind of church – more nearly a church of the poor, a church of the bible, a church of Jesus.

*Source*: Article by John Vincent in Haddon Willmer (ed), *20/20 Visions: The Future of Christianity in Britain*, SPCK 1992, pp. 65ff.

---

## 6. By offering an informed commentary on political affairs

Methodism must not imagine that it still lives in times like those when, it was said, cabinet ministers lay awake wondering what Hugh Price Hughes, founder of the West London Mission and editor of the *Methodist Times*, would say. In that sense, the days of the Nonconformist conscience are past, and no church can go it alone. But Christians can still act in the spirit of S. T. Coleridge who said that the universal church needs to be 'the sustaining, correcting, befriending opposite to the world, the compensating counterforce to the inherent and inevitable defect of the state'.[6] This means making astringent comments on the society and policies of the day in the light of our 'transformist' theology, while recognizing that we are a minority. We must not assume that people are mindless, unable to think for themselves; and it must be clearly understood that some Methodists dislike their leaders speaking for them when they have no mandate to do so.

One of the changes from the last generation is the declining number of Methodists in local government and civic life, though there are outstanding examples, like Peter Bounds, Chief Executive of Liverpool. The role of the early retired and of men and women in their sixties without the threat of redundancy needs exploring here. All in all, the wise words of Herbert Butterfield [89] need constantly to be pondered.

---

89. Along with that great defender of the Church of England, Lord Clarendon, we must sadly accept the fact that the affairs of the world would be worse off if we were governed by ecclesiastical statesmen. The Christian who feels that his religion has anything to contribute to the politics of today must realise that the outsider is going to be very cautious of him. He had better disguise his message as common sense.

*Source*: C. T. McIntire (ed), *Herbert Butterfield: Writings on Christianity and History*, OUP 1979, p. 78.

---

## 7. By committing itself unequivocally to mission

Methodism, at its best, has always seen church structures as determined by missionary needs. It has believed, in other words, that church polity is the handmaid to evangelism. There is always tension between concern to develop the life of the gathered community and the desire to see Christ enthroned at the heart of national life which we have called the 'transforming' emphasis. The emphasis finds expression in direct evangelism – the opening of the eyes to see Christ at work now – and mission alongside Christ's poor, and it makes use of the contribution both of black Methodists with their vigour, passion and sometimes radicalism, and of lay people at every level of national life.

The bare bones of such a position, which affects the whole Connexion, are clearly seen in a statement prepared by the Home Mission Division [90].

---

90. Christian Commitment to mission arises from God's care for his world. From the Bible in general and from Jesus in particular, we learn about God's love for the whole creation. By mission we mean any way in which Christians are sent to share in experiencing and expressing that love. It involves evangelism since God has declared his desire for all mankind to know and love him. It includes social caring for God's mercy reaches out especially for the poor and needy. It incorporates the political struggle for justice in our society because God intends men and women to live at peace together. These three do not exhaust the missionary task, neither are they alternatives in our mission, for they belong inextricably together. Indeed they should be areas of passionate commitment by us, since the world is so desperately far from what God intends in all three areas. They are imperatives, not options.

*Source*: *Sharing in God's Mission*, Methodist Church Home Mission Division 1985, p. 9.

---

## 8. By explaining and defending the Christian faith

Can we offer a reasoned case for Christian faith in a post-modernist world in danger of destroying the positive aspects of the Enlightenment? The importance and difficulty of tackling this question – the task known as 'apologetics' – should never be underestimated. But equally the possibilities in the Anglican–Methodist Quadrilateral, which has recurred through these pages, should not be forgotten.

*Scripture*, with Christ at its heart, is still for Methodists the prime source of Christian faith, and therefore evangelicals, catholics and radicals in our midst are united – in a way that needs exploring – in acknowledging that Christianity is a faith rooted in history. *Tradition* is the sum of Christian wisdom in response to the truth revealed in scripture. It both provides continuing guidance and enables us to share in the prayers of sixty generations of Christians! *Reason* was never for Wesley the source simply of a dry, rational moralism. Like the seventeenth-century writer, John Smith, he sees 'the truest knowledge of

God as that which is kindled within us by a heavenly warmth in our hearts' and affirms that 'that which enables us to know and understand aright the things of God must be a living principle of Holiness within us'.[7] We do well to explore the God-given discipline of ordering our thoughts as cogently as we can. *Experience*, in a broad sense, was the avenue by which, at the beginning of this century, Methodists began to explore theology. We need to recover it again. But as we sing of the 'wonder why such love for me' we must never forget the wisdom of the centuries or the authority of scripture.

Apologetics can be done at any level. An elderly lady once asked me, 'Why did my son have to die of asbestosis?' We were immediately into a discussion about creation and its misuse, capitalism, greed and ignorance as well as modern medicine. Or take the question 'Why didn't God stop the massacres in Rwanda?' Any answer must cover providence and human freedom and the judgment of God's non-intervention. Again, what answers have we to Richard Dawkins and the biologists who see everything in terms of DNA? And what of the enormous issues raised by bioethics? To think of any of this in purely denominational terms would be ludicrous, but the Home Mission Division was right to set up a Working Group to explore the issues [91].

Finally, we must not forget the enormous challenge of dialogue with men and women of other faiths which cannot be conceived in denominational terms and is too important a theme to be dealt with in a cursory manner.

## 9. By maintaining groups which can nurture faith

Evangelism is futile unless there are groups to nurture faith, helping people to grow and share Christian insights in the world. At a time when the 'basic Christian communities', small lay groups, are revolutionizing the life of Roman Catholicism in South America and elsewhere, Methodists do well not to indulge in vainglory, though small group spirituality was the chief characteristic of early Methodism. The lay-led 'Class Meeting' was not only a means of nurture – some detractors might say conformity to group norms – but of evangelism. It enabled searchers to become finders as well as helping the finders to become evangelistic. Wesley constantly had to say that the revival was a 'rope of sand' unless those reached by preachers like George Whitefield were gathered into groups. Today, of course, so many on the 'Second Journey' are aching for meaning that the rites of passage provide an enormous opportunity for compassionate evangelism. But groups, like a renewal of pastoral care for ministers and laity, are still essential to growth.

As E. R. Wickham acknowledged back in 1957 [92], the local church needs to foster 'face to face' groups which provide support and challenge to action, and Methodists, with their long tradition and wealth of experience in this area, have something invaluable to contribute.

---

91. In that quest, as William Temple once put it, 'I am not asking what will Jones swallow. I am Jones asking what there is to eat!' . . . [T]he search is for a faith which takes proper account of our tradition, is alive to development in biblical and theological understanding and can make sense of what is happening in the secular world. If it is possible we want to find authenticity and wholeness as contemporary Christians and to proclaim a gospel which is public truth for our time.

*Source*: Mervyn Willshaw introducing a collection of articles on 'Faith and the Way we live now' in the *Methodist Recorder*, 2 June 1994.

---

92. . . . there are conditions and needs to be fulfilled by the modern missionary project that were met in a quite remarkable way through the early Methodist organisation – notably in the 'class meetings'. Thus there is the need for smaller, warmer, more community-minded expressions of the Christian community than attendance at public worship alone can prove.

*Source*: E. R. Wickham *Church and People in an Industrial City*, Lutterworth Press 1957, p. 266. (Wickham was an Anglican bishop and founder of the Sheffield Industrial Mission.)

To some these nine points may seem to provide a limited agenda. There is much more, certainly, that is worthy of serious attention. But the areas on which we have focussed can constitute important elements in any continuing role which Methodism may play.

## The future

Let us sum up. What seems to us facile optimism, and indeed sometimes imperialism, typified the Methodism of 1900. Greater realism marked the period after the First World War. There was a brief period of renewed confidence after 1945. Then came the era of secularism, marked by a renewal of belief in political activism and a long courtship with Anglicanism. The failure of the Anglican–Methodist Unity Proposals in 1972 was followed by both a crisis in identity and a renewal of a sense of mission. Can Methodism now face the future in Britain with sober confidence? Do we face, in this country, a total collapse of theistic religion or is Diarmaid MacCulloch right to point to the future as belonging to the Pentecostal style of Christianity? 'In terms of sheer numbers', he says, 'they will probably soon become the chief representatives of the Western Christian tradition in the world.' But he also reminds us that 'For all the complexity of the two-thousand-year Christian story . . . we need to remember just how young an institution the Christian church is in the whole human story.'[8] Perhaps it is best to conclude with a passage from Gordon Rupp which puts all such speculation in the right perspective.

> The test of a living Church is how far it bears the form of a Servant, which is a hidden form known only by faith . . . The Church too is a hospital where bad people are made good, and sinners forgiven . . . The test is not whether the services are exciting, up-to-date, experimental or impressively alert to recent intellectual discussion. A tiny group of rather dull people in some down-town chapel, coping with raising inordinate sums of money to keep going a building with damp and peeling walls, unappetizing and off-putting, may still reveal all the hidden majesty of God, be where Grace is offered. I am all for experiments, for lovely new churches, for fine music, for exciting and moving liturgy. But I know that in the moment when a man's sins have found him out, or when he has to face the fact of cancer, all these things are almost completely irrelevant.[9]

## For discussion

1. Is there any reason why the establishment of the Church of England should continue?
2. What shape do you think future worship and preaching in Methodism should take?
3. Do you think ten networks of people to share their work insights could be formed ecumenically in your area?
4. Do we need new communities of Christians in the inner cities? Would you want to join one? Why? Why not?
5. How should our church relate to national politics?
6. What does evangelism mean to you? What does your church do to offer the gospel?
7. 'God! How can we believe in God with so much suffering in the world?' How would you answer that person's agonizing question?
8. What do you think the job of your minister ought to be? Do we require ordained ministers at all?
9. Are you optimistic or pessimistic about the future of church or world?
10. What will the millennium mean for you?

# Notes

*Preface*

1. E. J. Hobsbawn, *Age of Extremes: The Short Twentieth Century, 1914–1991*, Michael Joseph 1994, p. 3.

*1. Introduction*

1. J. Plumb, *England in the Eighteenth Century*, Penguin 1969, pp. 93f.
2. R. Moore, *Pit-men, Preachers and Politics*, CUP 1974, p. 116.
3. Ibid., p. 142.
4. H. J. Perkin, *The Origins of Modern English Society 1780–1880*, Routledge & Kegan Paul 1969, pp. 340ff.
5. D. Hempton, *Religion and Popular Culture in Britain and Ireland*, CUP 1996, p. 46; G. Milburn, 'Piety, Profit and Paternalism', *Proceedings of the Wesley Historical Society*, December 1983, p. 66.

*2. Methodism 1932–1950*

1. Cited by R. N. Flew, 'Methodism and the Catholic Tradition' in *Northern Catholicism* ed N. P. Williams and C. Harris, SPCK 1933, p. 528.
2. Adrian Hastings, *A History of English Christianity 1920–1990*, SCM Press 1991, p. 464.
3. This description is based on the memoirs of Dr J. T. Wilkinson (1893–1980), later Principal of Hartley Victoria College, who was a minister in a notable succession, including Dr Herbert G. Marsh (1889–1991) who wrote a significant book on Baptism.
4. Alan Wilkinson, *Dissent or Conform?*, SCM Press 1986, pp. 29–82.
5. G. T. Brake, *Policy and Politics in British Methodism 1932–1982*, Edsall 1984, pp. 683ff.
6. Hastings, op. cit.

*3. Methodism 1950–1998*

1. Hastings, op. cit., pp. 465, 549.
2. In 1996, the college became Mission in Business, Industry and Commerce (MIBIC) and will be a kind of mobile Academy as part of the 'Church and Society' sector in the new Methodist structures: see box 20 and associated text.

*4. Methodism and the Wider World*

1. Cf. D. W. Brogan, *The English People*, Hamish Hamilton 1943, p. 121.
2. S. Koss, *Nonconformity in Modern British Politics*, Batsford 1975, pp. 187ff.
3. See A. Wilkinson op. cit., p. 169.
4. B. L. Manning, *More Sermons of a Layman*, Independent Press 1944, p. 37.
5. Professor M. Howard, 'Attitudes to War', *The Observer*, 15 November 1970.
6. See O. Chadwick, *Michael Ramsey*, OUP 1990; reissued SCM Press 1998, pp. 241ff.
7. J. W. de Gruchy, *The Church Struggle in South Africa*, Collins 1986.
8. J. M. Bonino, *Revolutionary Theology Comes of Age*, SPCK 1975 and *Christians and Marxists: The Mutual Challenge of Revolution*, Hodder & Stoughton 1976.
9. Owen Chadwick, *The Christian Church in the Cold War*, Allen Lane 1992, p. 35.
10. Cited, without further detail, by A. Marwick, *British Society since 1945*, Penguin 1982, p. 196.

*5. The Methodist Emphases Today*

1. Lesslie Newbigin, *Honest Religion for Secular Man*, SCM Press 1966, p. 30.

2. *Journal of the Revd Charles Wesley: The Early Journal 1736–1739*, Culley 1909, pp. 134–35.
3. Gonville ffrench Beytagh, *Encountering Darkness*, Collins 1973, p. 254.
4. Address to the Methodist Conference, 1976.
5. Dag Hammarskjøld, *Markings*, Faber 1964, p. 108.
6. Malcolm Muggeridge, *Something Beautiful for God*, Collins Fontana 1972, p. 49.

## 6. *Methodist Worship and Preaching*

1. David Martin, *The Sociology of English Religion*, Heinemann 1967, p. 88.
2. See D. H. Tripp, *The Renewal of the Covenant in the Methodist Tradition*, Epworth Press 1969.
3. D. H. Tripp, art. 'Methodism' in C. Jones, G. Wainwright and others, *The Study of Liturgy*, revd edn SPCK 1992, p. 325.
4. Erik Routley, *Into a Far Country*, Independent Press 1962, p. 131.
5. J. E. Rattenbury, *Vital Elements in Public Worship*, Epworth Press 1936, 3rd edn 1954, p. 114.
6. See Bibliography.
7. See Bibliography.
8. See *Methodist Service Book* (1975), section 6 above and box 54.
9. For the place of Local Preachers, see G. Milburn and M. Batty (eds), *Workaday Preachers*, Methodist Publishing House 1995.

## 7. *Methodism and the Wider Church*

1. For details of these negotiations see: J. M. Turner, *Conflict and Reconciliation: Studies in Methodism and Ecumenism in England, 1740–1982*, Epworth Press 1985, chs 9 and 10; Owen Chadwick, *Michael Ramsey*, OUP 1990; reissued SCM Press 1998, pp. 333ff; Adrian Hastings, *Robert Runcie*, Mowbray 1991.
2. See *Called to be One*, Churches Together in England (CTE) Publications 1996.

## 8. *Methodism – Youth and Age*

1. As, for example, in *Growing Christians*, BCC 1957, p. 4.
2. See *Preparation for Service: a scheme of minimum requirements for all who take up work on behalf of the church among children and young people*, Methodist Youth Department 1972.
3. Westhill College, the Free Church College of Education in Selly Oak, Birmingham, made very important contributions at this time.
4. Cyril Garbett, *Preface to the Agreed Syllabus of the East Riding Council*, cited in *Church, Child and School*, Free Church Federal Council 1960, p. 11.
5. See D. S. Hubery, *Teaching the Christian Faith Today*, Methodist Youth Department 1965; H. F. Mathews, *Revolution in Religious Education*, Religious Education Press 1966.
6. The Lindsey (Lincolnshire) Religious Education Syllabus was one of the most celebrated 'Agreed Syllabuses' used in Day Schools after the 1944 Education Act.
7. London Weekends were annual events for young people, combining dramatic presentations, sports events, comedy, discussion and worship. They still take place but their format is now under review: see *Methodist Recorder* 21 and 28 August 1997.
8. The *Albemarle Report*, a government sponsored survey, advocated much greater civic involvement in youth work through Local Education Authorities.
9. *Charter 95*, a report sponsored by MAYC and acclaimed by the Methodist Conference, advocates radical changes in worship styles, music, church life, evangelism and ministry.
10. Adrian Hastings, *The Shaping of Prophecy*, Geoffrey Chapman 1995, p. 71.
11. John Walsh, Profile of W. R. Ward, 'Methodist Historian and Historian of Methodism', *Epworth Review*, September 1995, pp. 41–42.
12. Frederic Greeves, *Theology and the Cure of Souls*, Epworth Press 1960, p. 150.
13. Grace Davie, *Religion in Britain since 1945: Believing without Belonging*, Blackwell 1994. An important book.
14. The *Robbins Report* of 1963 led to the creation of a clutch of new universities and polytechnics.
15. *Easter People*, led by the Revd Dr Rob Frost, offers an annual vibrant, evangelistic, holiday-style week, involving drama, workshops, new styles of worship and fun, with the aim of renewal and outreach.
16. This prayer was written by the Revd David Reddish, Chairman of the Bolton and Rochdale District, for the *Methodist Prayer Manual*, 1995 to mark the 50th anniversary of MAYC.

## 9. *Methodist Scholarship*

1. Murray's book was a 'Fernley-Hartley' lecture, a label which merits some explanation. Lectures, usually résumés of work later printed in book form, were delivered at both the Wesleyan and Primitive Methodist Conferences. They were designed to stimulate ministerial theological reflection and were sponsored by John Fernley and Sir William P. Hartley respectively. The hyphenated title is thus a result of Methodist Union in 1932. Though perhaps not well known outside Methodism, the importance of these lectures – before and after Union – should not be underestimated. Indeed, the distinguished Free Church historian, Dr Geoffrey Nuttall, told me that they provide striking illustrations of changes in British theology. Thus in this century they have moved from stress on religious experience, through biblical theology and the clear influence of Karl Barth, to much wider themes.

2. Adrian Hastings, *The Theology of a Protestant Catholic*, SCM Press 1990, p. 190.

3. D. E. Nineham, *St Mark*, Penguin Books 1963, p. 12.

4. For an appreciation, see Introductory essays by A. Raymond George and C. Leslie Mitton in Vincent Taylor, *New Testament Essays*, Epworth Press 1970, pp. 1–30.

5. The historian Herbert Butterfield warns that 'the question of our religion must never be regarded as merely a matter of historical evidence . . . it is wrong to assume – as people often do when they are dealing with the scriptures – that if an event has not been demonstrated with mathematical certainty, it has been proved not to have happened at all', C. T. McIntire (ed), *Herbert Butterfield: Writings on Christianity and History*, OUP 1979, pp. 109–110.

6. See Bibliography.

7. Vincent Taylor, *Jesus and His Sacrifice*, Macmillan 1937, p. 322.

8. See G. W. Anderson, 'Norman Henry Snaith', *Epworth Review*, January 1986.

9. See G. S. Wakefield, *Robert Newton Flew*, Epworth Press 1971.

10. See J. M. Turner, 'Gordon Rupp as Historian', *Epworth Review*, January 1991.

11. Basil Willey, *Christianity Past and Present*, CUP 1952, p. 1.

12. See Leslie J. Griffiths, 'A Tribute to Basil Willey', *Epworth Review*, May 1985.

13. Basil Willey, *More Nineteenth Century Studies*, Harper Torchbook 1966, p. 9.

14. See D. and E. Hawkin, *The Word of Science: The Religious and Social Thought of Charles Coulson*, Epworth Press 1989.

15. See J. M. Turner, 'The Christian and the Study of History: Sir Herbert Butterfield', *Proceedings of the Wesley Historical Society*, February 1987.

16. For the content of this paragraph, see Herbert Butterfield, *Christianity and History*, Bell 1949, pp. 54, 58, 146; and *International Conflict in the Twentieth Century*, Routledge & Kegan Paul 1960, p. 32.

## 10. *Methodism and the Future*

1. R. E. Davies, *Methodism*, Penguin 1963; 2nd edn Epworth Press 1985.

2. J. S. Habgood, *Church and Nation in a Secular Age*, Darton, Longman & Todd 1983, p. 105; and *Making Sense*, SPCK 1993.

3. B. L. Manning, *Essays in Orthodox Dissent*, Independent Press 1939; Daniel Jenkins, *The British, their Identity and their Religion*, SCM Press 1975; Adrian Hastings, *Church and State – The English Experience*, Exeter University Press 1991.

4. Quoted without further identification in J.-J. von Allmen, *Worship, its Theology and Practice*, Lutterworth Press 1965, p. 13.

5. See Robin Gill, *Prophecy and Praxis*, Marshall, Morgan & Scott 1981.

6. S. T. Coleridge, *The Constitution of the Church and State* (1839 edn), pp. 124f.

7. Cited from John Smith, *Select Discourses* (1673) in P. L. More and F. L. Cross, *Anglicanism*, SPCK 1957, p. 223.

8. D. MacCulloch, *Groundwork of Christian History*, Epworth Press 1987, pp. 293, 297.

9. E. G. Rupp, *The Old Reformation and the New*, Epworth Press 1967, p. 62.

# Bibliography

*of books mentioned but not quoted, and therefore not detailed in footnotes*

T. Beeson, *Discretion and Valour*, Collins 1974

Herbert Butterfield, *The Whig Interpretation of History*, G. Bell 1931, 1950
   *The Statecraft of Macchiavelli*, G. Bell 1940, 1955
   *The Englishman and His History*, CUP 1944
   *The Origins of Modern Science 1300–1800*, G. Bell 1949
   *George III, Lord North and the People*, G. Bell 1949
   *Christianity and History*, G. Bell 1949
   *Man on his Past*, CUP 1955, 1969
   *The Origins of History*, Eyre Methuen 1981

David Clark, *Between Pulpit and Pew*, CUP 1982

*Companion to the Lectionary* series, Epworth Press:
   D. Calvert and J. Stacey, vol 1, *Prefaces to the Lessons* (1982)
   A. Dunstan and N. Ellis, vol 2, *Hymns and Anthems* (1983)
   Neil Dixon, vol 3, *A New Collection of Prayers* (1983)
   Christine Odell, vol 4, *Prayers of Intercession* (1987)
   Peter Sheasby, vol 5, *All Together for Worship* (1994)
   Michael Townsend, vol 6, *Worshipping God Together* (1996)

John de Gruchy, *Christianity and Democracy*, CUP 1995

Gregory Dix, *The Shape of the Liturgy*, Dacre Press 1945

Gregory Dix (ed), *Catholicity: A Study of the Conflict of Christian Traditions in the West*, Dacre Press 1947

W. F. Flemington, *The New Testament Doctrine of Baptism*, SPCK 1948

R. N. Flew and R. E. Davies, *The Catholicity of Protestantism*, Lutterworth Press 1950

R. N. Flew, *The Idea of Perfection in Christian Theology*, OUP 1934
   *Jesus and His Church*, Epworth Press 1938

K. Grayston, *Dying We Live: a new enquiry into the death of Christ in the New Testament*, Darton Longman and Todd, 1990

Kenneth Greet, *The Big Sin*, Marshalls 1982

F. Greeves, *Theology and the Cure of Souls*, Epworth Press 1960

J. H. Hick (ed), *The Myth of God Incarnate*, SCM Press 1977

Richard Hoggart, *The Uses of Literacy*, Penguin 1958

H. Maldwyn Hughes, *The Theology of Experience*, Kelly 1915

William James, *The Varieties of Religious Experience*, Longmans Green 1902ff.

T. E. Jessop, *Social Ethics, Christian and Natural*, Epworth Press 1952
   *The Christian Morality*, Epworth Press 1960
   *An Introduction to Christian Doctrine*, Nelson 1960

Alan Kay, *The Nature of Christian Worship*, Epworth Press 1953

K. E. Kirk, *The Vision of God*, Longmans Green 1931; Harper Torchbook 1966

John Lawson, *Green and Pleasant Land*, SCM Press 1955

Local Preachers Department, *Doctrinal Preaching*, 1951

Caryl Micklem (ed), *Contemporary Prayers for Public Worship*, SCM Press 1967
   *More Contemporary Prayers*, SCM Press 1970
   *Contemporary Prayers for Church and School*, SCM Press 1975

J. H. Moulton, *Religions and Religion*, Kelly 1913

A. Victor Murray, *Personal Experience and the Historic Faith*, Epworth Press 1939

H. D. Rack, *Reasonable Enthusiast: John Wesley and the Rise of Methodism*, Epworth Press 1989

A. M. Ramsey, *The Gospel and the Catholic Church*, Longmans Green 1936; SPCK 1990

John Robinson, *Honest to God*, SCM Press 1963

Edward Rogers, *A Christian Commentary on Communism*, Epworth Press 1951

E. G. Rupp, *Luther's Progress to the Diet of Worms*, SCM Press 1951
   *The Righteousness of God*, Hodder & Stoughton 1953

C. Ryder Smith, *The Christian Experience*, Epworth Press 1926

Norman H. Snaith, *The Distinctive Ideas of the Old Testament*, Epworth Press 1944

Vincent Taylor, *The Historical Evidence for the Virgin Birth*, OUP 1920
   *Behind the Third Gospel*, OUP 1926
   *The Gospels*, Epworth Press 1930
   *The Formation of the Gospel Tradition*, Macmillan 1933
   Trilogy on Atonement:
   *Jesus and His Sacrifice*, Macmillan 1937
   *The Atonement in New Testament Teaching*, Epworth Press 1940
   *Forgiveness and Reconciliation*, Macmillan 1941
   Trilogy on Person of Christ:
   *The Names of Jesus*, Macmillan 1953
   *The Life and Ministry of Jesus*, Macmillan 1954
   *The Person of Christ in New Testament Teaching*, Macmillan 1958
   *The Gospel according to St Mark*, Macmillan 1952

J. Neville Ward, *The Use of Praying*, Epworth Press 1967

Philip S. Watson, *Let God Be God*, Epworth Press 1947

Geoffrey Wainwright, *Christian Initiation*, Lutterworth 1969

*Eucharist and Eschatology*, Epworth Press 1971

*Doxology*, Epworth Press 1980

Geoffrey Wainwright, C. Jones and others, *The Study of Liturgy*, 2nd edn SPCK 1992

*The Study of Spirituality*, SPCK 1986

Leslie Weatherhead, *Discipleship*, SCM Press 1934

Basil Willey, *The Seventeenth Century Background*, Chatto & Windus 1934; Penguin 1964

*The Eighteenth Century Background*, Chatto & Windus 1940; Penguin 1965

*Nineteenth Century Studies*, Chatto & Windus 1949; Penguin 1969

*More Nineteenth Century Studies*, Chatto & Windus 1956; Harper Torchbooks 1966

*Christianity Past and Present*, CUP 1952

*Religion Today*, A. & C. Black 1969

Frances Young, *Sacrifice and the Death of Christ*, SPCK 1975; SCM Press 1983

# Suggestions for Further Reading

This is not an exhaustive book list. The aim is to give necessary background information. Shorter books, which are more suitable for general reading, are marked with an asterisk.

## General introductions: twentieth-century background

Noel Annan, *Our Age: The Generation that Made Post-War Britain*. Fontana 1991
> An evocative book about the intelligentsia. The only Methodists mentioned are Lord Soper and Sir Herbert Butterfield!

D. Childs, *Britain since 1939*, Macmillan 1995*
K. Robbins, *The Eclipse of a Great Power. Modern Britain*, Longmans 1992
E. J. Hobsbawn, *Age of Extremes: The Short Twentieth Century 1914–1991*, Michael Joseph 1994; Penguin 1995
> Hobsbawn is a brilliant and provocative Marxist.

A. Marwick, *British Society since 1945*, Penguin 1982*
J. Stevenson, *British Society 1919–1945*, Penguin 1984*
A. J. P. Taylor, *English History 1914–1945*, OUP 1965
D. Thomson and G. Warner, *England in the Twentieth Century 1914–1979*, Penguin 1991*
Peter Clarke, *Hope and Glory: Britain 1900–1990*, Allen Lane 1996

## Church history: useful introductions

G. Davie, *Religion in Britain since 1945*, Blackwell 1994*
S. Gilley and W. J. Sheils (eds), *A History of Religion in Britain*, Blackwell 1994
Adrian Hastings, *A History of English Christianity 1920–1990*, SCM Press 1991
> Hastings is a Roman Catholic and highly perceptive. A brilliant survey.

Gerald Parsons, *The Growth of Religious Diversity, Britain from 1945*:
  vol 1, *Traditions*, Routledge 1993
  vol 2, *Issues*, Routledge 1994
T. Thomas (ed), *The British: Their Religious Beliefs and Practices 1800–1986*,
  Routledge 1988*
B. G. Worrall, *The Making of the Modern Church: Christianity in England since
  1800*, SPCK 1988*


*On Methodism since 1932*

G. Thompson Brake, *Policy and Policies in British Methodism 1932–1982*, Edsall
  1984
    Exhaustive detail on Conference statements and controversies. Useful
    correctives at times to establishment blandness.

R. E. Davies, A. R. George and E. G. Rupp (eds), *A History of the Methodist
  Church in Great Britain*, vol 3, Epworth Press 1983, esp. chapters 3, 4, 8, 9, 10
R. E. Davies, *Methodism*, 2nd edn Epworth Press 1985
    Still a 'classic' but needs supplementing

R. E. Davies, *Methodism and Ministry*, Methodist Publishing House 1993*
    A personal view 'from the top'

R. E. Davies (ed), *The Testing of the Churches 1932–1982*, Epworth Press 1982
  (esp. ch. 2, 'Methodism')*
The Methodist Church, *Declarations on Social Questions*, Epworth Press 1959
The Methodist Church, *Declarations and Statements on Social Responsibility*,
  Methodist Publishing House 1981
The Methodist Church, *Statements on Social Responsibility 1946–1995*, Meth-
  odist Publishing House 1995
The Methodist Church, *Declarations of Conference on Faith and Order
  1933–1983*, Methodist Publishing House 1984
Other Conference Reports 'adopted' or 'received' by the Methodist Conference
will be found in the *Agenda* of Conference for that year. Many are available as
separate pamphlets from the Methodist Publishing House, 20, Ivatt Way,
Peterborough, PE3 7PG or from Methodist Church House, 25, Marylebone
Road, London NW1 5JR

J. M. Turner, *Conflict and Reconciliation: Studies in Methodism and Ecumenism
  1740–1982*, Epworth Press 1985, chs 9 and 10


*Biographies are a good way in. Try –*

E. C. Urwin, *Henry Carter OBE*, Epworth Press 1952
D. and E. Hawkin, *The Word of Science: The Religious and Social Thought of
  C. A. Coulson*, Epworth Press 1990

G. S. Wakefield, *Robert Newton Flew 1886–1962*, Epworth Press 1971

M. Wakelin, *J. Arthur Rank, 1888–1972: The Man Behind the Gong*, Tauris 1996

D. Gowland and S. Roebuck, *Never Call Retreat: a biography of Bill Gowland*, Chester House 1990

W. F. Lofthouse and others, *Wilbert F. Howard*, Epworth Press 1954

R. E. Davies (ed), *John Scott Lidgett*, Epworth Press 1957

John Walsh (ed), *A. B. Sackett*, Epworth Press 1979

John H. Lenton, *Harold Roberts*, Methodist Publishing House 1995

P. Sangster, *Dr Sangster*, Epworth Press 1962

B. Frost, *Good Will on Fire: Donald Soper's Life and Mission*, Hodder & Stoughton 1996

E. H. Robertson, *George: a biography of Viscount Tonypandy*, Marshall Pickering 1982

G. Thomas, *Memoirs of Viscount Tonypandy*, London 1985

J. A. Newton, *A Man for All Churches: Marcus Ward*, Epworth Press 1984

K. Weatherhead, *Leslie Weatherhead*, Hodder & Stoughton 1975

R. G. Burnett and others, *Frederick Luke Wiseman*, Epworth Press 1954

# Index

*Figures in parentheses after a page number indicate more than one reference on that page.*